THE A–Z OF INDEPENDENT SCHOOL LEADERSHIP

GUY HOLLOWAY

SERIES EDITOR: ROY BLATCHFORD

Together we unlock every learner's unique potential

At Hachette Learning (formerly Hodder Education), there's one thing we're certain about. No two students learn the same way. That's why our approach to teaching begins by recognising the needs of individuals first.

Our mission is to allow every learner to fulfil their unique potential by empowering those who teach them. From our expert teaching and learning resources to our digital educational tools that make learning easier and more accessible for all, we provide solutions designed to maximise the impact of learning for every teacher, parent and student.

Aligned to our parent company, Hachette Livre, founded in 1826, we pride ourselves on being a learning solutions provider with a global footprint.

www.hachettelearning.com

Although every effort has been made to ensure that website addresses are correct at time of going to press, Hachette Learning cannot be held responsible for the content of any website mentioned in this book. It is sometimes possible to find a relocated web page by typing in the address of the home page for a website in the URL window of your browser.

Hachette UK's policy is to use papers that are natural, renewable and recyclable products and made from wood grown in well-managed forests and other controlled sources. The logging and manufacturing processes are expected to conform to the environmental regulations of the country of origin.

To order, please visit www.hachettelearning.com or contact Customer Service at education@hachette.co.uk / +44 (0)1235 827827.

ISBN: 978 1 0360 0506 1

© Guy Holloway 2025

First published in 2025 by
Hachette Learning (a trading division of Hodder & Stoughton Limited),
An Hachette UK Company
Carmelite House
50 Victoria Embankment
London EC4Y 0DZ
www.hachettelearning.com

The authorised representative in the EEA is Hachette Ireland, 8 Castlecourt Centre, Dublin 15, D15 XTP3, Ireland (email: info@hbgi.ie)

Impression number   10 9 8 7 6 5 4 3 2 1
Year   2029 2028 2027 2026 2025

All rights reserved. Apart from any use permitted under UK copyright law, no part of this publication may be reproduced or transmitted in any form or by any means, electronic or mechanical, including photocopying and recording, or held within any information storage and retrieval system, without permission in writing from the publisher or under licence from the Copyright Licensing Agency Limited. Further details of such licences (for reprographic reproduction) may be obtained from the Copyright Licensing Agency Limited, www.cla.co.uk

Typeset in the UK.
Printed in the UK.

A catalogue record for this title is available from the British Library.

CONTENTS

Dedication v
About the author vi
Acknowledgements and thank you vii
Foreword by Roy Blatchford viii
Introduction x

Section One

Advertising 3
Boarding 11
Culture 19
Discipline 25
Eton 31
Finances 37
God 45
Heart 51
Inequality 57
Juggling 63
Kindergarten 73
Latin 81
Magpie 87
Networking 93
Oomph 99

Parents 105

Quirkiness 113

Reflectiveness 119

Safeguarding 125

Trust 131

Unity 137

Vocation 143

Wellbeing 149

Xenophilia 153

Yesteryear 159

Zeitgeist 165

Section Two

1. Politics and independent education 173

2. Sleep – the case for later school starts 179

3. Financial competency for independent school leaders 183

4. Answers to asides 187

References 189

Further reading 191

to Jasmine
who taught me about love

ABOUT THE AUTHOR

Guy Holloway is the co-founder and former headmaster of Hampton Court House, an independent co-educational school in West London. He read English at Peterhouse, Cambridge, where he spent three years working with children in local authority care through Save the Children. He then lived in Paris, working in public relations before 'falling into' teaching. Guy began his career at Ecole Active Bilingue, where he taught O-level and A-level English. He was part of the founding team of the Harrodian School in 1993 and co-founded Hampton Court House in 2001.

An advocate for bilingual education and cultural immersion, Guy is known for exposing his pupils to the fullest range of music, art and literature. He has written widely on education, served as a 'leading thinker' with the National Education Trust (2013–18), and lectured on educational leadership at the Institute of Education (2014–18).

A regular media commentator, Guy has appeared on Sky News, BBC, ITV and numerous radio programmes to discuss educational reform, particularly his campaign for later school-start times for teenagers, supported by Oxford University's Sleep and Circadian Neuroscience Institute.

He is also a patron, alongside Sir Anthony Seldon, of Their Future Today, a charity supporting and educating abandoned children in Sri Lanka.

Guy lives in London, continues to write for *School Management Plus* and other journals, and runs a China–UK education business with his wife Jasmine.

ACKNOWLEDGEMENTS AND THANK YOU

To the thousands of pupils and parents from whom I have learned so much – especially those who have spoken truth to power, offering the kind of constructive feedback that helped make our school a better place for all.

To all my teaching colleagues across the world over the past 35 years – and especially to everyone at Hampton Court House, where for twenty years we truly were a family.

To the friends and fellow educators with whom I've regularly exchanged ideas – including those early morning conversations on LinkedIn!

To the following, who contributed in various ways to this book: Alastair Campbell, Anne-Françoise Ropert, Duncan Murphy, Ian Smith, Irfan Latif, James Harding, Jonathan Taylor, Matthew Burke, Rachel Bowles, and Tom Arbuthnott.

Finally, my thanks to the three people who have most shaped my leadership and personal development: Dr Max Coates, formerly of the Institute of Education, who for years has championed my ideas with wisdom and generosity; Tristram Jones-Parry, who supported my headship with unfailing kindness and confidence; and Roy Blatchford CBE, who as Director of the National Education Trust opened up countless new educational vistas, and whose belief in me helped bring this book into being.

FOREWORD

Like people, independent schools come in all shapes and sizes, making it difficult to group them under a single label. While they are sometimes referred to as 'private' schools, this term has largely fallen out of use within the sector in the UK owing to the unhelpful connotations of exclusivity and secrecy. The term 'public school', once commonly used but always a misnomer to our American friends, has also fallen into abeyance.

Meanwhile, many preparatory schools – traditionally educating boys until age 13 – have been forced to rethink their business models in response to changing times, for example by becoming co-educational and/or educating to the age of 11 only. This process of evolution and reinvention is set to continue, as the market adjusts to the challenges posed by the introduction of 20% VAT on school fees in the UK from January 2025.

School budgets can vary widely, from modest turnovers of a few hundred thousand pounds to fee incomes well north of £50 million in the case of larger boarding schools. But even that pales in comparison to the billion-dollar, for-profit, private-equity-backed education groups that have been scrambling in recent years to buy up schools in the UK and indeed across the world.

International education giants such as Nord Anglia and GEMS Education have set new benchmarks in the field, joined by fast-growing organisations like Cognita, Inspired Education Group, Dukes Education and others. The result has been a dramatic transformation of the UK's educational landscape. Today's independent schools are increasingly sleek, professionally managed and expertly marketed; a far cry from the days of the small, eccentric, proprietor-owned or family-run schools – though some wonderful exceptions remain.

Boarding schools are inevitably in intense competition for the limited number of UK-based families able to afford the fees. In response to a dwindling domestic market, these schools have adopted sophisticated global-marketing strategies to attract international students in order to survive – a move that would have been unimaginable just a few decades ago.

Moreover, many prestigious British schools have expanded their influence and soft power by licensing their names to international partners. Their heads and senior leaders now frequently jet off to other continents, further strengthening ties between the original institutions and their growing family of satellite schools.

Meanwhile, political criticism of independent education at home has grown, with the sector facing intense scrutiny over its perceived inequalities. Yet, paradoxically, our liberal British independent education model is widely celebrated abroad and remains a significant export. In this context, leaders of independent schools must not only steer their own place of learning but also be prepared to act as public champions for the sector as a whole.

****

In common with other titles in the A–Z series, Section One is organised around the 26 letters of the English alphabet, with the Asides offering intriguing quizzes for intellectual amusement. Section Two provides a range of resources by way of advice, provocation and reflection.

Guy Holloway is a distinguished educator who knows the independent, international and state education systems very well. His fluency takes the reader on a spirited and highly readable journey from **Boarding** and **God**, through **Magpie** and **Oomph**, to **Xenophilia** and **Yesteryear**.

Enjoy the ride, *wherever* in the world you teach children and young people. This is truly a book for teachers and leaders in any sector, in any context.

Roy Blatchford, series editor

INTRODUCTION

Independent schools can be remarkable, even magical, places. They transform children's lives by creating environments where education is truly personalised – tailored to each pupil's unique needs and talents. And it's worth noting that over a third of all pupils at independent schools receive some form of fee assistance, with nearly 10,000 pupils across the UK paying no fees at all.

However, no school's survival is guaranteed in challenging times. At their core, independent schools are businesses, subject like any other enterprise to market forces. Deeply held educational ideals must be balanced with the practical realities of financial sustainability – and yet a wise and compassionate leader understands that not every initiative needs to be profitable. This nuanced interplay between vision and viability lies at the core of all exceptional leadership in independent schools.

This A–Z guide is aimed primarily at leaders within the independent sector, though it may also appeal to professionals in state education – whether they are considering a move to independent schools or seeking a deeper understanding of how the sector operates.

As always, context is key; what works for one school may not suit another. So please pick-and-mix ideas or discard them entirely as they come along! But whether you are grappling with issues of financial sustainability, managing parent relations or leading staff through periods of change, the text offers reflections, advice and, most importantly, encouragement.

Few would dispute the fact that the UK's education system, despite its strengths, needs reform. We certainly need to attract more high-quality teachers and leaders to our noble profession. A central theme of this book is that independent schools, with their vast collective knowledge and experience of looking at issues from outside the box, have a critical role to play in driving innovation and change.

My hope is that this book will inspire current and future leaders *in both sectors* to reflect, challenge assumptions and to innovate for the benefit of all children across the UK, now and in the future.

Guy Holloway

SECTION ONE

ADVERTISING

From the wide-eyed wonder of reception to the poignant farewells at the Year 13 leavers' ball, those of us who work in education are privileged to witness life in all its beauty, fragility and promise.

But alongside this magic lies a cold fact: your independent school is a business. And you are a service provider. Without a steady stream of pupils and parents who believe they are receiving return on investment, the books won't balance. In recent years, numerous fee-paying schools have closed; today's economic and political landscape is tougher than ever, and only the most responsive will survive and thrive.

THE NUMBERS DON'T LIE

Even with an outstanding education on offer, a fee-paying school is likely to struggle without an effective advertising culture. The independent schools that flourish today as businesses recognise that a top-notch marketing and communication strategy is as vital as delivering a first-rate service. The two are inextricably linked.

NOT A DIRTY WORD

Let's reclaim the true meaning of the word 'advertising'. In education, it should have nothing to do with slick sales patter. The Latin root of the word *advertere* means 'to turn towards' or 'to direct one's attention to'. Advertising isn't just necessary – it's the lifeblood of the school.

An effective leader instils pride in all staff – teaching and non-teaching – in delivering a premium Rolls-Royce-level service. This pride should extend from answering emails promptly to comforting a young child after a fall. Every interaction with the parent body and wider community is an opportunity to advertise the school's values. The cumulative effect is that parents notice, talk and spread the word. Your current parents are by far your most powerful ambassadors. Providing personal attention and demonstrating that you know their children as individuals are the surest ways to grow your school. One influential parent can lead to two, five, or more, families enrolling.

From the warmth of the receptionist's greeting to the pride a security guard takes in welcoming visitors, these small moments leave a lasting impression. Yet, some schools fail spectacularly in this regard. For example, one headmaster's secretary, known locally as 'the dragon', tightly controlled access to the head. Her stern demeanour and unapproachable manner made for amusing gossip but likely contributed to the prep school's declining numbers.

Successful advertising isn't about spending exorbitant sums; nor can it compensate for a poor product. It must be woven into the very DNA of the school. A strong public image, a genuine commitment to sharing facilities and expertise, and meaningful community engagement should all be part of the plan.

A PARENT'S JOURNEY

Parents choosing independent education are making one of the most significant financial and emotional investments of their lives. You can't simply 'sell' to them with a generic school video or with the head's tired pitch about 'nurturing the whole child'.

A parent engages in careful research, heartfelt conversations and considerable soul-searching. The most successful heads and registrars understand the anxieties associated with every stage of a parent's journey:

- **Awareness**: A parent first hears about your school, ideally through word of mouth, but perhaps via a well-placed advertisement, a schools' fair or even just driving by. At this stage, your online presence matters immensely. Prospective parents will look you up, so check review sites like Mumsnet regularly, and scrutinise your social media.

- **Enquiry**: The parent reaches out via email, phone or an online form. Make it easy for a parent to do this. Quick, personalised follow-ups are essential. In a small-to-medium-sized school, a warm phone call often works better than an acknowledgement by email. Every interaction should be curated, with details like family dynamics, siblings and hobbies noted for future personalisation.
- **Engagement**: Parents visit the school for a tour, perhaps attend some lessons or come to an open day. These experiences must be authentic and not a show 'put on' for parents. Ideally, *every* day is run as 'an open day' and it therefore matters that displays are tidy, classrooms are well-presented and that adults and pupils move around with cheerful purpose. This is by far your best advertising, so nurture daily the things that make your school a joyful place to be. After the visit, follow up personally, preferably by phone, to strengthen the connection. Seek genuine feedback about the impressions.
- **Assessment**: Independent schools that pride themselves on being non-selective are adept at designing straightforward and stress-free admission processes that focus on welcoming and valuing the child as an individual. You can be sure that parents will tell their friends about how you've handled the process! In a selective school, it is essential that the process is clearly and transparently laid out. Invariably, there will be some kind of entrance test, either in the form of written papers or an online adaptive test. But it is during the interview process that you can truly 'advertise' the values of your school. How are visiting children and their parents received at the school? Regardless of the outcome, how do you ensure that visitors have a positive experience? Opinions differ regarding interviews, but inviting parents into the head's office alongside the child can serve as another opportunity to showcase the school's ethos.
- **Reputation**: Before making a final decision, a parent is likely to consult with friends, asking, 'Have you heard of such-and-such a school? What do you think of it?' The process of buying education has, for better or worse, a certain social cachet. Some parents are confident enough to choose a school just because they like it. But most will want to have their choice validated by their social circle, confirming that they are doing the right thing, or at least that they are not doing a foolish thing.

- **Decision**: After deliberation, parents either entrust their child to you or look elsewhere. While the paperwork might resemble a business transaction – complete with terms and conditions, accepting the term's notice before withdrawal – what's actually happening is quite different. It is an act of trust that no school leader should ever take for granted. In the days when parents sent in a cheque, I would hold it with a certain humility, keenly aware of what it represented – a parent's faith that I would nurture and care for their precious child to the very best of my ability. The day one loses sight of this is the day one loses the human touch.

For selective schools, rejecting an applicant requires sensitivity. A tactful rejection letter, offering constructive feedback and keeping the door open for a future application, can turn a difficult moment into a positive experience. On one occasion, we turned a child down, with detailed feedback and a recommendation to another school (with whom we were on good terms). The neighbour then visited with her child, saying, 'I'd like to enrol my child because I saw the concern you showed for the child next door whom you didn't accept, so I'd love to know what you do for one you do accept'.

THE HEAD AS BRAND MANAGER

In small-to-medium-sized schools, the head is the face of the brand. Some heads excel at using social media, sharing glimpses of school life, giving a thoughtful online assembly or participating in memorable traditions – like singing Flanders and Swann or jumping into a lake at the end of the summer term! These moments communicate the school's ethos and get people talking. (You can be sure that parents will share these anecdotes and video clips with friends and family.) Parents want to know who will guide their child's education and whether the head is approachable, competent and inspirational.

During my own headship, I often sent brief, personal emails to parents following interactions with their children. After chatting with Alice in Year 2 about her new art project, I'd drop a quick note to her parents sharing how delightful our conversation had been. These weren't fabricated; they were true moments of connection. And I tried to send one such email most days – and, in particular, targeting those shyer, less-ebullient children who might otherwise be overlooked. These genuine gestures of connection built trust and goodwill, but also turned parents into enthusiastic advocates for the school.

WORD OF MOUTH

Word of mouth is the most effective form of advertising. Parents trust recommendations from other parents far more than any brochure or website.

Conversely, disgruntled parents can cause serious damage. A single, well-connected parent can influence several others to reconsider their choices. Addressing concerns promptly mitigates the risk of negative word of mouth. If the worst happens, parting ways with a family respectfully, without ill will and without ego is a skill that heads must develop.

STANDING OUT

In a crowded field, focus on what genuinely sets your school apart. Perhaps you offer something unique or distinctive, like lessons in Sanskrit, a specialist Singaporean maths programme or a quirky tradition that your community cherishes. Lean into these strengths for they are what make your school memorable.

When it comes to pastoral care, show – don't just tell. Use anonymised, real-life examples to bring your ethos to life: the school refuser who found their way back to the classroom; the painfully shy child who stole the show on stage. Every school will have such stories. And while you're at it, showcase your inclusive ethos, and evidence how you support personal development and leadership. Parents want to see not just promises but proof.

RESULTS

For very many parents, proven examination success at GCSE and A-level remains the most convincing reason to choose an independent school and is a clear indicator of return on investment. If strong results are your calling card, don't be shy about leading with them.

Of course, everyone in education knows that the most academically successful schools – state and independent – are also the most selective. But even so, this should not stop a school from celebrating and then using these results to attract more bright children. It is a tried-and-tested formula that works.

Where you can *really* shine, though, is by showcasing your value-added performance. Even if you aren't topping the league tables for raw exam results, you might be leading the way in how much progress your students make during their time with you. Value-added data can be a game-changer in marketing campaigns, offering a compelling measure of your school's impact.

PRACTICAL TIPS

- Maintain a professional, easy-to-navigate website.
- Invest in SEO (search engine optimisation) to boost online visibility.
- Plan memorable, authentic open days.
- Use social media thoughtfully and consistently.
- Engage with the local community and with both national and local media, positioning your school as a centre of educational debate.
- Prioritise attention to detail; a tidy, well-maintained school site speaks volumes.
- Always follow up personally after visits or enquiries, and keep following up.

MEASURING SUCCESS

Always track key metrics like enquiry-to-enrolment ratios and compare year-on-year data. Use customer relationship management (CRM) software or a detailed spreadsheet to keep organised. Analysing this data allows you to refine your strategy and allocate resources effectively. But remember that your advertising budget is only as effective as the quality of your school, and the effectiveness of the follow-through process, right up to the point of enrolment.

FINAL THOUGHTS

Advertising a school is about so much more than flashy campaigns, marketing bumph and online ads. It's about positioning your school as a forward-thinking, connected and reflective hub of educational thought and debate. What matters is what others say about you – from current and former parents to other heads, other schools and the wider community. Their opinions carry far more weight than any brochure or marketing spiel. It's about building coherence, trust and authenticity; showing a genuine commitment to doing your best for your students and striving to make the world a better place.

It's about the small, consistent, everyday moments of communication and impression-making. It's about showing true care for your students and their families – because they will always be your most powerful and authentic ambassadors.

ASIDE

WHO AM I?

1. I am the fictional headmistress of a girls' boarding school in Cornwall.
2. At the beginning of each school year, I invite all the new girls into my office, telling them, 'I count as our successes those who learn to be good-hearted and kind, sensible and trustable, good, sound women the world can lean on.'
3. I have seen many girls grow from mischievous or insecure children into confident, capable young women.
4. My school is located by the sea, and the setting plays an important role in the girls' adventures and personal growth.
5. The series in which I appear follows one year group, from first form to sixth form, but I remain a steady and respected presence throughout.

BOARDING

Gone are the days when seven-year-olds were dropped off at the start of term and collected at the end. Gone are the days when enduring boarding school was considered a character-building rite of passage for the British elite. Though, if we're honest, a whiff of this lingering attitude still permeates a few corners of society, not least among some of the survivors.

Today's boarding landscape has transformed dramatically. Our schools have reimagined their model entirely and serve as a template for British-style boarding schools across the world. Co-education is now the norm, students stay connected to home via technology (in a controlled way at designated times) and many boarding schools offer flexible options from weekly boarding to regular exeats and flexi-boarding arrangements.

One prep school head, Tom Rogerson, recently shared on social media a stunning photograph of Cottesmore School with the following caption:

> The Ides of March well behind us and scholarship season nearly finished, we have started playing cricket already, between the last hockey matches. Summer might as well be here.
>
> The air smells sweet. The daffodils are lighting up the lawns. The mowers are already working overtime. The boys and girls are building dens.
>
> Nothing compares to it.

This vivid writing paints an English boarding school as a pastoral idyll – a Forest of Arden – offering refuge from the pressures facing today's youngsters. It presents itself as the antidote to a world where parents work excessive hours while children navigate TikTok, harmful online environments and other digital toxins. The head's values shine through: come children and build dens!

This is independent education in action because while educationalists earnestly discuss curriculum reform, one head can bypass all this with what is truly important: freedom, spontaneity, connection with nature and the magic of childhood. This same small school is known for leading the way on AI – hosting conferences bringing together eminent educationalists and experts. In short, a boarding prep school punching above its weight, at the cutting edge of educational debate, yet not losing sight of what matters most.

> **TIP**
>
> Short, authentic social-media content can be used to showcase your school's magic effectively. A quick TikTok or Instagram video of everyday moments often communicates far more than a polished promotional film ever could.

THE BOARDING ADVANTAGE

Being part of a boarding community offers a richness that cannot be fully appreciated unless you've lived it. For the right child in the right school, it can be transformative.

- A place (not a 'space') with laughter, warmth and round-the-clock care.
- A focus on wellbeing with onsite matrons, nurses and counsellors.
- A safe haven from the algorithmic rabbit holes that plague today's youth.
- Structure around technology use, with mainly phone-free experiences.
- More of those 168 weekly hours spent profitably in work and play.
- Exceptional opportunities to develop character, resilience and teamwork.
- Time to pursue sports, music and arts, often to a high standard.

- Time to stand and stare.
- A vertical house system creating unique social dynamics.

FINANCIAL REALITY CHECK

Let's be frank; quality round-the-clock care is expensive. Unless parents can access bursaries, boarding remains eye-wateringly costly for most families.

That said, for professional parents working in major cities, coordinating nannies, school buses, after-school clubs and other expenses can sometimes add up to roughly the same cost as boarding – particularly weekly boarding. For some families, weekly boarding improves everyone's quality of life.

> **TIP**
>
> Help prospective parents to understand the full cost comparison. When they factor in all the hidden costs of city living with children, boarding might be more accessible than they initially assume.

INTERNATIONAL DIMENSION

The 'Harry Potter' phenomenon and the heady economic conditions of the early 2000s saw a significant uptake in domestic boarding. But today, the home market is dwindling, and many schools depend heavily on international enrolment – with some reaching up to 30% or more of Chinese students, particularly in sixth forms.

Without international students from China, Germany, Russia, Ukraine, Nigeria, the US and beyond, most UK boarding schools would struggle to survive. Most schools employ agents who scour the globe in search of students. Some fly their heads out to give presentations, emphasising personal care and academic success.

This international dimension creates a mini United Nations where teenagers form lifelong friendships across continents. By embracing this reality, schools offer richer, more-diverse experiences for all students.

The internationalism should work both ways. If you have a sizeable contingent from Nigeria, Taiwan or any other country, you should aim to develop meaningful knowledge of that country – its politics, culture, food and history. Make conversations about students' home countries a regular practice.

Some schools excel at cultural exchange, while others adopt a passive 'we need you here' approach. Remember, also, that international students may face immense pressure to perform academically and appear happy regardless of their actual experience.

HOUSEPARENTS

The happiness of your boarders largely comes down to the exceptional personal qualities of your housemasters and housemistresses. They become the main point of contact for both students and parents.

These crucial roles demand extraordinary human qualities that few day-school teachers can fully appreciate. Their primary responsibility is noticing: reading emotions, detecting problems early and providing support before issues escalate.

The best housemasters and housemistresses:

- set the tone and culture of the entire house
- command respect while maintaining warmth
- function seamlessly in the background
- handle emergencies at any hour
- function effectively on limited sleep
- maintain their sense of humour
- laugh at the occasional absurdities of boarding life.

Leadership priorities with regard to houseparents

Your school's reputation and success hinge on these pivotal roles. If you are in senior leadership, continually ask yourself, 'What more can we do to support our houseparents?'.

- Show deep respect. While senior leadership might nominally run the school, it would collapse without these key figures.

- Ensure their working conditions are as favourable as possible, with scheduled time off properly covered by competent deputies. You'll need actively to develop younger staff to learn the ropes and imbibe the culture of your school, to create a supply of future houseparents.
- Ensure their salary (not just their 'package') reflects the exceptional work they do. Be as generous as finances allow. This is not an area to skimp on.

STAFFING AND 24/7 RESPONSIBILITY

Your boarding school is only as good as your staff. When hiring, look for experience in boarding environments as a starting point, but focus primarily on emotional resilience and character – you can train for specific skills later.

A 'this-is-not-in-my-job-description' mentality cannot work in a boarding community. Success relies on acceptance of a different working model with different rewards.

Unless you've experienced it firsthand, it's difficult to convey the sense of responsibility that comes with having children and teenagers under your care around the clock. Your first duty is safeguarding. Remember that your parent body will likely be articulate, aware of their legal rights and have the means to take action if things go wrong.

Staff retention is crucial, particularly for housemasters and housemistresses. Develop staff who might stay the course for 10 or 15 years or more in important roles.

TIP

Create clear communication channels with parents that establish expectations from the beginning.

SAFEGUARDING: THE NON-NEGOTIABLE

From a leadership perspective, providing a sound academic education must come a very clear second to ensuring a safe environment for every student in your care.

Boarding schools face additional safeguarding risks, including the vulnerability of young international students far from home with language and cultural barriers.

Discipline requires absolute clarity. You must be firm, fair and consistent – which may mean permanently excluding pupils for serious misconduct. Be crystal clear about boundaries and be prepared to follow through.

Scrutinise student applications carefully. Ask direct questions about suspensions, discipline records, maturity and family support. Be prepared to decline admission if the fit isn't right. Be especially careful with mid-year applications and sixth-form entries where one bad apple may cause mayhem. Sometimes a school will try to offload a troublesome student to a smaller, more-financially-pressed school. Beware!

SPECIAL CONSIDERATIONS

Schools with large international contingents must make serious efforts to understand those cultures – not just take the money. Consider appointing a bicultural staff member on your leadership team if you have a significant number of students from a particular country.

An important concern is the lack of regulation around educational guardians (required for visa applications) for international students. As a minimum, UK schools should insist on seeing DBS (Disclosure and Barring Service) checks for guardians, though currently this isn't required by law.

> **TIP**
>
> Consider recommending guardianship agencies accredited by AEGIS (the Association for the Education and Guardianship of International Students) or the certified guardian scheme of the Boarding Schools' Association (BSA).

WHEN THINGS GO WRONG

Stories of historical abuse in boarding schools continue to emerge. These must never be forgotten, and the most dangerous attitude is assuming 'all that was in the past'. Today's boarding schools have invested heavily in safeguarding, but vigilance remains essential.

Hire media relations specialists *before* you need them. In a crisis, you don't want to be scurrying around looking for one. If facing a serious situation where abuse has occurred:

- be open about what happened and how the school responded
- create a transparent culture that always investigates concerns
- never brush anything under the carpet.

THE FUTURE

The future of any boarding school lies in its ability to tell its authentic story and connect emotionally with prospective families. Modern boarding can position itself as a solution to contemporary problems – offering structure around technology use and genuine community in an increasingly fragmented world.

For the right child in the right school, boarding remains a transformative experience unlike any other educational opportunity. Your job is to create that environment, protect it fiercely and communicate its value in a world that increasingly needs what boarding, at its best, can offer.

> ## ASIDE
> ### WHO AM I?
> 1. I was born in South Africa but spent much of my career in Britain, where I became a prominent figure in education and literature.
> 2. My early life was shaped by political activism, and – to the best of my knowledge – I am the only HMC (The Heads' Conference) headmaster to have served time in prison.
> 3. After leaving South Africa, I became an educator in the UK, working in some of the country's most prestigious independent schools.
> 4. Beyond my role in education, I was also a poet and novelist, often reflecting on themes of exile, identity and resistance.
> 5. I never lost my connection to the struggles of my homeland, writing extensively about South African history and politics.

CULTURE

To what extent do members of staff in your school read, discuss and exchange books *in addition* to delivering their classroom lessons? When was the last time you overheard teachers passionately debating a book, exhibition or concert in the common room? Do they swap or recommend novels to each other? We can't 'teach' culture exactly – but we can oxygenate the water in which we all swim by fostering an atmosphere where these things matter.

Some cultural reference points feature, of course, in prescribed exam syllabuses: Bartók's *Concerto for Orchestra* in GCSE Music, *The Strange Case of Dr Jekyll and Mr Hyde* in GCSE English Literature, or a mention of Hobbes' *Leviathan* in A-level Politics. But how can a school go further? How can a school ensure that students and staff alike are immersed in the sweep of our cultural history?

And though it makes sense to focus more on the Western canon, reflecting our geography, let's introduce where we can elements from African, Asian, Ottoman and other cultures too. Not because it is fashionable or elitist to do so, but because acquaintance with our collective cultural heritage – its music, art, literature and political thought – is essential to understanding ourselves and the world we live in.

BEYOND THE SYLLABUS

School leaders are compelled to tick the boxes of inspection criteria (Independent Schools Inspectorate (ISI) and Ofsted) to meet the standards that define an 'outstanding' school. How can we evidence learning? Has the assessment objective been met? And all that. Yet we all know that a cultured person is not one who has passed a test. How many students have studied *Othello* to achieve a top grade at GCSE, only to never read another word of Shakespeare again? Clearly that's not a success.

First-rate examination results can be achieved, even by students of modest ability, by teaching the mark schemes. Naturally, the best teachers resist this reductionism, and the most-memorable lessons are often those that, propelled by intellectual curiosity, veer thrillingly off track; where a literary reference leads to an unexpected detour into art history, or a philosophical question opens the door to political theory. These are the moments where education transcends the merely functional. But for this to happen, you need to give your staff the freedom to fly – in and out of the classroom.

APPOINTING STAFF

When recruiting, seek these core key qualities in a classroom teacher:

- reflectiveness and self-awareness
- a deep subject knowledge (which needs to be tested at interview)
- a strong classroom presence
- a commitment to students' emotional and intellectual growth.

To these, add a fifth: cultural literacy. When choosing between two equally qualified candidates, the decisive factor should be their intellectual breadth. The preferred candidate is the one who has read more widely, possesses broader knowledge and nurtures passions beyond their specialist field.

All schools have a duty to foster a *culture of reading* – but how can this be done if teachers themselves don't read? Students must see their teachers reading, discussing ideas and recommending books. The titles on a teacher's desk can spark curiosity more effectively than any formal reading list. As I write this, I'm fondly remembering my French teacher (who much preferred Russian) and who, during lessons, would stand in front of the class and read us reams of Lermontov. ('You don't need to understand the Russian', he'd say, 'just hear how beautiful it is.')

TEACHERS' PASSIONS

When teachers share their passions, students absorb cultural capital by osmosis. Readers of a certain generation may recall the heyday of *Grange Hill* in the early 1980s (script-edited by none other than Anthony Minghella). In one episode, Mr Baxter, the PE teacher, takes a cover English lesson; the fourth-formers titter when he enters the classroom and asks what they are studying. But to their surprise, Baxter beams with delight as he flips through the pages of the class reader, exclaiming,

> 'Drayton, Marlowe, Shakespeare – my word! It's wasted on you bunch of Philistines of course!'
>
> (YouTube, *Grange Hill*, series 6, episode 14)

Drayton! When teachers transcend their subject and reveal something of themselves, an extraordinary cross-pollination occurs, leaving indelible marks on both heart and mind.

INFORMAL LEADERSHIP

Culture need not always be highbrow. Consider this eminent boarding school head who emailed his students on the third Monday in January:

> Dear all,
>
> The third Monday in January is supposedly the morale low point of the year. In true Harrovian fashion, I hope you've defied it.
>
> For a Mancunian who grew up in the 1980s, Blue Monday means something quite different.
>
> [followed by a YouTube link to *Blue Monday* by New Order]

In one quick email, he'd shared a slice of music history, some cultural geography (Manchester's music scene) and connected with both staff and students. No curriculum time required.

POETRY

Few educational practices shape emotional and intellectual sensibilities as powerfully as learning poetry by heart. Consider that phrase: *by heart*. If something is to be imprinted there, should it not be worthy?

Tennyson's *The Charge of the Light Brigade* ('Theirs not to reason why') may be unfashionable today, but it conveys more about nineteenth-century Britain than many a PowerPoint. Or how about Wordsworth's *The Tables Turned* ('Come forth into the light of things/Let Nature be your teacher') which remains as relevant as ever.

Even pupils in Year 1 can learn Blake's *The Fly* while discovering his vivid paintings. They can even learn *The Sick Rose*, even if its meaning is not yet fully formed in their minds. The resonance of such verses lingers, subtly shaping their own writing and self-expression.

And one crucial point – if pupils are expected to learn poetry by heart, so must their teachers. English teachers, in particular, should embody the practice they advocate.

VISITING YOUR SCHOOL

What does a walk through your school reveal? Do your corridors shimmer with intellectual life? Or are your displays intended to showcase regulatory compliance with rehearsed phrases about fundamental British values?

Are there books on desks, posters of famous paintings, quotations from political thinkers? Are students exposed to new ideas simply by being present? A manga artist here, a new word there, a Rosalind Franklin display up there. Some schools you visit for an hour and you leave enriched. Others feel barren. The difference is not funding but ethos. A cultural school does not bolt on enrichment; it lives it – in every corridor, every classroom, every conversation.

GENERAL KNOWLEDGE

The brilliant form tutor who begins each morning with three quick-fire general knowledge questions isn't just filling time – they're building neural networks. A central bank of general knowledge questions, spanning music, history, literature and science and used in tutor time or house competitions, gives students a web of reference points. Investing in quiz buzzers (or commissioning some from the DT department) adds a whole new layer of extracurricular learning.

BEYOND THE CURRICULUM

One of the great advantages of an independent education is the freedom to experiment and design new courses of study. For years I taught my own Cultural Studies class to my Year 10s. One lesson a week. No exams. But over three terms we read Prévost's *Manon Lescaut*, and explored Ibsen, Marx, Freud, and Germaine Greer. It was a jigsaw of ideas, slowly taking shape, connecting disciplines that are too often kept in separate boxes. Students initially bewildered soon began bringing in their own cultural connections ('this reminds me of that *Black Mirror* episode', and so on).

A history teacher was an expert in Byzantine history. Cue – Year 9 studied the Byzantine Empire, while eking out contemporary geopolitical parallels. It played to the particular idiosyncrasies of this one teacher – a man widely considered to be 'inspirational' – but, arguably, the strength of the course was not *what* was taught, but rather the emotional charge of *how and why* it was taught.

Of course, innovation is not confined to independent schools. Katharine Birbalsingh, head of Michaela Community School, wrote an open letter to the Education Secretary, Bridget Phillipson, in 2025, decrying a curriculum so rigid that it drives creative teachers from the profession:

> There needs to be a broad academic core for all children. But a rigid national curriculum that dictates adherence to a robotic, turgid and monotonous programme of learning that prevents headteachers from giving their children a bespoke offer tailored to the needs of their pupils, is quite frankly, horrifying. Anyone in teaching who has an entrepreneurial spirit, who enjoys thinking creatively about how best to address the needs of their pupils, will be driven out of the profession. Not to mention how standards will drop! High standards depend in part on the dynamism of teachers.

Whether one works in the state sector or the independent sector, the responsibility remains the same: to empower staff to be cultural leaders. Let them design short courses. Let them lead their students to draw their own connections between disciplines.

SURVIVAL

In our current reality of algorithmic bubbles, deepfakes and industrial-scale misinformation, cultural literacy isn't a luxury – it's armour.

A student who has wrestled with Orwell understands doublespeak when they see it in political discourse. One who has studied propaganda posters can identify emotional manipulation in social-media campaigns. A teenager who has responded emotionally to *Romeo and Juliet* will recognise impulsivity in their own decision-making.

Our shared common culture matters more than ever. In an age of AI and with infinite knowledge at our fingertips, we risk drowning in information while starving for sense. Developing cultural literacy gives students a filter, a compass, a sensibility – moral, intellectual, aesthetic – that enables them to judge, discern and delight. How else to distinguish between the algorithmically generated and the authentically human?

So, I'll ask one more time – what place does culture have in your school? Is it something taught, or something lived? Is it confined to subjects labelled 'arts' or does it flow through every conversation, corridor and classroom? Because culture isn't just about knowing things – it's about finding meaning.

ASIDE

WHO AM I?

1. I was born in Vienna in the late nineteenth century, into a family that revolutionised psychology.
2. While my father explored the unconscious mind and dreams, I focused on defense mechanisms and how children develop psychologically.
3. My most influential work was with war-traumatised children, especially those affected by World War II in London.
4. I wrote extensively on ego psychology, focusing on how children develop resilience and manage anxiety.
5. My work laid the foundation for child therapy, influencing modern approaches to psychological care and education.

DISCIPLINE

This chapter is an attempt to offer a few thoughts on discipline in schools. I'm treading carefully because, over the years, I've visited many hundreds of schools – state and independent – in the UK, and many dozens in Europe and Asia. Some of these schools, especially in Asia, have been, to my mind, rather too hierarchical and yet I've been struck by how courteous students are, by how everyone moves with purpose, and the real sense of momentum you can feel in these places. Staff and pupils are happy, achieving and safe.

And take one UK prep school with deeply 'traditional' practices – pupils standing when you enter, strict uniform enforcement (top button done up, tucked shirts) and every sentence ending with 'Sir' or 'Miss'. That school's discipline also translates into considerable sporting and academic success.

We don't need, in the independent sector, a one-size-fits-all approach. Part of the justification for the existence of independent schools is that we provide parental choice. It's a near-ideal situation when values align between home and school, as parents and the school can then work together in partnership effectively. The sector's strength lies in offering diverse educational experiences that match different family preferences.

REFRAMING DISCIPLINE

For some, discipline means authority, punishment, even humiliation. But let's not forget its etymology (again from the Latin): *discere* – to learn; *discipulus* – a pupil. Discipline isn't about control; it's about learning. It's about the training – mental, emotional, even physical – that enables someone to pursue their goals. It's what makes freedom possible, whether that's being a Premier League footballer or a neurosurgeon. And this is how we need to talk to children and teens about discipline; not as something that is done to them, but rather something that will help them get to wherever they want to go.

DISCIPLINE IN SCHOOL

The little things matter, whether it's a student slouching in their chair, a teenager breezily walking in five minutes late or a coat thrown on the floor. These small signs of disengagement are often overlooked, but they should not pass unchecked. Setting the tone and getting these things right are part of the atmosphere of learning.

Each lesson needs to start clearly and promptly. Any disruptive behaviour must be called out – gently, if possible, and with a light touch. Posture and tone communicate far more than words ever can. School leaders should always observe body language when on learning walks. (It's remarkable what you can tell even from a distance or through a window.) Consider investing in body language and communication training for staff members to enable them to strengthen these classroom-management skills.

As a school leader, your voice is an instrument and it is a good idea to practise from time to time in an empty room. Can you enunciate well enough to throw your voice to the back of the room without raising your voice? What different registers can you find in your voice? Do you have an actor friend who can give you some voice exercises? This is well worth investing in. Your presence, how you stand, your body language and your voice are all part of what makes you an effective teacher and leader. There may well be times when you will feel you need to raise your voice – but do this judiciously; it must be a tool that you *choose* to employ. You never raise your voice in anger, for you are always in control.

If members of the school leadership team can't control their emotions, it affects how others behave too. If, as a senior leader, you want a calm, orderly, respectful school, you must model that behaviour daily. You simply cannot afford emotional outbursts.

The DfE document 'Behaviour in Schools: Advice for headteachers and school staff' (2024) has a section on 'Responding to misbehaviour', but there is nothing here about prioritising time to build relationships with students. Instead, teachers should 'respond assertively in accordance with the school behaviour policy'.

A behaviour policy is a legal requirement for all schools and is usually downloadable from the school's website. These documents vary in tone. The policies of an increasing number of independent schools reflect practice in the state sector, and thus you will read of 'the rewards we use and the sanctions we adopt'. But the policies of some independent schools are tonally quite different, for they stress the building of strong relationships and the importance of trying to understand the underlying causes of any disruptive behaviour, before venturing down the path of sanctions.

Any policy is only as good as its implementation – not just whether it is uniformly applied, but crucially *how* it is applied. One of the most important things we can do as school leaders and teachers is to stop *reacting* and start *responding*. When a pupil rolls their eyes, or is just plain rude, we are often tempted to make it all about us. 'How dare they do that!', we think. But we've chosen to be teachers, to work in this challenging profession. Our job is to care about our students – but not to make our caring conditional on their behaviour! Arguably we need to care *more* when a student is rude or disruptive. There are times when we just have to leave our ego at the door.

Bad behaviour almost always stems from underlying issues: stress, confusion, home difficulties or a cry for help. Our job is to respond thoughtfully and effectively, not react. During critical moments, we maintain 'unconditional positive regard' while staying calm, consistent and kind.

Find time to speak with the student privately, not with an accusatory 'explain yourself' approach, but from a genuine desire to understand and connect. Create a safe space where they feel comfortable sharing what's really going on.

This approach works; it really works in nearly all cases. The issue, however, is time. In the end, this is a leadership decision about the kind of school you want – control the students with rewards and sanctions, or dispense with that and focus on building trusting relationships. Both methods work – but you get a different kind of school depending on which you choose.

CONVERSATION

Most misbehaviour, in my experience, can be addressed through genuine, caring conversation. Not a telling-off; not a five-minute lecture; but a real, human conversation. Provide a safe space for students to speak and to be heard.

As the American educationalist Rita Pierson famously says in her 2013 TED talk – 'Every kid needs a champion'. Be prepared to invest time in these cases. Moving to the next stage of your behaviour policy might achieve a short-term result, but if the student hasn't been heard, you're not addressing the core issue.

Sometimes I've shared my own school struggles in these conversations. What matters is being fully present; showing genuine support while validating the student's worth (for typically, self-esteem is low). You're building bridges, always separating the behaviour from the person.

With younger pupils especially, it is important to involve parents, though they may need gentle guidance. Remind parents not to be overly harsh with their children. The goal is to build trust between parent and school – and a loving circle of care around the child.

As an aside and general observation, there is a correlation between children who lie effortlessly and children who have had overly strict homes or schooling. Such children have learned through disproportionate punishment that admitting fault is dangerous. Your job is to help them unlearn this narrative and show that accepting responsibility demonstrates character strength – a path that leads to genuine respect, trust and *belonging* in your school community.

RELATIONSHIPS FIRST

There's no doubt that behaviour policies, tracking software and classroom apps can help. They can bring consistency and provide evidence. But they cannot replace human connection. A teacher who repeatedly logs sanctions without actually speaking to or listening to the student misses a crucial opportunity.

Instead, we should ask: How well do I know this student? Have I had a proper conversation with them recently? Do I understand what's happening in their life outside my classroom? Have I created a safe, non-judgemental space for them?

And perhaps more provocatively: does our implementation (or partial implementation, or non-implementation) of behaviour policies help us build relationships – or does it sometimes hinder them?

WHEN THE SYSTEM ISN'T WORKING

If you have the same students in detention week after week, it's time to ask yourself whether your approach actually changes anything. Because if a sanction doesn't change behaviour, it's not a sanction – it's just a ritual.

Sometimes, counter-intuitive solutions work best. I recall a constantly disruptive Year 3 pupil; he was clearly bright but disengaged. After discussing with his parents, we moved him up a year. It was risky, but he thrived in his new class. He needed challenge, not punishment.

What about the seemingly irresponsible teenager? Could they be given responsibility instead? Perhaps they could help to coach younger students in football. Being trusted often becomes the first step towards becoming trustworthy. Every good school has stories where out-of-the-box thinking – not an escalation of sanctions – turned a life around.

CONSEQUENCES ARE NECESSARY

This isn't a call for softness. There are, of course, non-negotiables. Bullying, racism, sexual harassment, protected characteristics, dishonesty – these must be dealt with clearly, and with a seriousness that shows you are protecting your community. But even then, we can act gently, and if sanctions are imposed, always in sorrow. And we can make space for redemption. ('I know you can learn from this – this is the beginning of the new you.')

Sometimes, yes, a pupil will need to leave, for their own good and for the good of others. But that point should come at the end of a long, thoughtful road.

EVERY SCHOOL IS DIFFERENT

Culture matters. A school's approach to discipline must reflect its ethos. I've seen 'strict' institutions that excel because they're consistent and fair. I've also seen more relaxed, nurturing schools thrive because they invest deeply in relationships. There's no single right approach.

And remember, you can never be certain you have the full picture of a student's circumstances. Proceed with caution and respect. Be prepared to commit for the long term. You might be exactly the teacher this student needs – perhaps the only one with the particular skills to make a meaningful difference in their life.

ASIDE

WHO AM I?

1. I run a grim, poorly maintained boarding school 'where there are no holidays', where discipline is harsh and education is barely an afterthought.
2. I have a wife and son who share my unpleasant disposition and assist me in running my institution.
3. I teach spelling phonetically, thus 'w-i-n, win, d-e-r, der, winder, a casement. When the boy knows this out of book, he goes and does it.'
4. I frequently abuse my power, delighting in punishing children, especially those who dare to question me.
5. My cruelty is eventually exposed when a young, idealistic man comes to work for me and challenges my authority.

ETON

Eton! Just the mention of the name evokes images of tailcoats, top hats and centuries of establishment privilege. We can't entirely shake off Eton's history, which undeniably speaks of aristocratic dominance and a certain 'effortless superiority'. The college has educated countless prime ministers, archbishops and leaders of every stripe – alongside the occasional bounder or cad – yet over the last two decades, the college has reinvented itself to a remarkable degree.

Herein lies a problem. Media and public opinion frequently conflate Eton with independent education as a whole, reducing a diverse sector of over 2500 schools to stereotypes of starched collars and Latin prayers. This oversimplification distorts reality and ignores both the vast majority of independent schools that look nothing like Eton and the work Eton itself is undertaking in social mobility and outreach.

DISPELLING MYTHS
Let's start by dispelling some persistent misconceptions.

Myth 1: Eton is for the privileged few, and you need to register your child at birth
False! Like other senior schools, Eton uses an online adaptive admissions test in multiple-choice format; it is one of the most rigorous and meritocratic admissions processes in the country and Eton takes into account each candidate's exact date of birth. This pre-test, taken by boys in Year 6, identifies potential rather than privilege and isn't easily gamed by excessive tutoring. The school's annual intake of over 250 pupils comes from more than 110 different schools, including state primaries.

Myth 2: You need to attend a fee-paying prep school and study Latin and Greek to be offered a place

Wrong! Boys are assessed at age 10 through the computerised Independent Schools Examinations Board (ISEB) adaptive Pre-Test, that includes English, mathematics, verbal reasoning and non-verbal reasoning. Boys come from increasingly diverse backgrounds spanning state, independent and international schools. The days when an elite group of preparatory schools dominated Eton's admissions are long gone.

Myth 3: Etonians all come from wealthy, privileged families

No! The College spends almost £10 million annually on its bursary provision. About 270 of Eton's 1300 students receive substantial financial aid, with over a hundred boys attending completely free of charge. Over the last 20 years, Eton has taken forthright steps to diversify its community further with an absolute commitment to inclusivity – often facing considerable opposition from some older Etonians.

Myth 4: Eton epitomises the British class system and is socially exclusive

For over a decade, Eton has partnered with a range of state schools (notably Holyport College, a state boarding school), sharing facilities, teachers and expertise. With five other independent schools, Eton co-sponsors the renowned sixth-form college London Academy of Excellence, where a third of their 150 Oxbridge offers have gone to students eligible for free school meals. In total, Eton has coordinated over 1000 cross-sector partnerships between schools, charities and other organisations working together for student and teacher benefit. Yet your average journalist, radio presenter or social-media commentator seems blissfully unaware of this, as Eton is forever trotted out as shorthand for private school, ivory tower privilege.

SOCIAL MOBILITY

One of the most significant recent initiatives is Eton's partnership with Star Academies to create three sixth-form colleges in Middlesbrough, Dudley and Oldham. The aim is to give students from disadvantaged backgrounds their best shot at securing top A-level results and places at leading universities.

Eton's expertise provides not just coveted teaching positions, but administrative support, creating centres of excellence in these areas. Eton is putting its money where its mouth is by pledging £1 million a year into this scheme.

A UK BRAND

Unlike many big-name UK schools, Eton hasn't licensed its name internationally. You won't find Eton Shanghai, Eton Bangkok or Eton Dubai. The school could easily have cashed in many times over, but has remained steadfastly committed to maintaining its presence within the UK and furthering partnerships with the state sector.

Few schools have done more to signpost their direction of travel. Under the leadership of Tony Little and now Simon Henderson, Eton has demonstrated through concrete actions its belief that it has both a moral as well as an educational purpose. There is no future in preserving a bubble for the elite – this is now fully understood across nearly all schools in the independent sector.

BUILDING BRIDGES

This is a time for all independent school leaders to reach out and connect with their state counterparts for genuine two-way learning and understanding. Too much is made of the supposed antagonism between the 93% in state education and the 7% in independent education (a narrative that serves lazy journalism and political agendas). In reality, many parents move their children back and forth between the sectors, and those in independent sixth forms are more like 15%. Teachers increasingly cross between sectors, from state to independent and vice versa, enriched by their experiences.

Many readers will be familiar with the fourth principle in Stephen R. Covey's *The 7 Habits of Highly Effective People*:

> Seek first to understand, then to be understood.

If government, universities, researchers, teachers, unions and school leaders from both state and independent sectors could prioritise seeking first to understand, the UK could forge a truly world class education for all, drawing on our collective expertise and experience. The independent sector as a whole is fully committed to engaging with state education, learning from and appreciating its challenges. At the same time, independent school leaders must continue to serve as thoughtful advocates for their own educational approach, contributing their voice to the national conversation.

Currently, independent schools face the concerning prospect of being sidelined from national education debates owing to ideological differences. This exclusion comes alongside the dual challenges of punitive taxation measures and a government that appears reluctant to engage meaningfully with the sector.

ACTION POINTS

- **Assess your community impact**. How does your school benefit local schools and neighbourhoods? Organise events for nearby schools, share facilities and develop partnerships. Learn from other schools which do this well.
- **Strengthen inclusion efforts**. Ensure your bursary programme reaches those most in need. Are you communicating opportunities effectively? Can you raise additional funds for assisted places? Review your application processes to remove hidden barriers.
- **Engage with national priorities**. Stay informed about educational debates. Share data (e.g. from the Independent Schools Council) on the independent sector's enormous economic contribution to the UK. Participate in curriculum reform, oracy initiatives and special needs advocacy. Visit state schools and organise joint activities. Work actively to dismantle the 93%/7% divide and challenge the 'four legs good, two legs bad' mentality.

THE PATH FORWARD

Today's risk is that productive partnerships will end for political reasons, sacrificing the benefits of cross-sector collaboration. We must engage with government at all levels and challenge the notion of an unbridgeable divide between state and independent sectors.

Given the current challenges, some schools may be tempted to pull up the drawbridge, focusing exclusively on families that can afford the fees, while aggressively marketing to wealthy overseas families. This would be a profound strategic error, as the advances of recent years must be sustained and developed.

CONCLUSION

Eton College, like many independent schools, has acknowledged its moral obligation to wider society. Eton can justifiably claim that it has led the way, pioneering initiatives that promote social mobility and share expertise across sectors. If all other independent schools follow suit, even in small ways or so far as their means and resources will allow, then the battle for educational equity might indeed be won on the playing fields of Eton, transforming a symbol of privilege into a catalyst for positive change.

ASIDE

WHAT SHORT STORY AM I?

1. I was written by one of the most famous British short-story writers of the twentieth century, known for his dark humour and twist endings.
2. My narrator is a middle-aged, routine-obsessed commuter who takes the same train to work every day.
3. As the narrator observes a new passenger, he becomes convinced that it is his old tormentor from school, now grown respectable.
4. I explore themes of power, trauma and the long-lasting effects of childhood cruelty in the English boarding schools of yesteryear.
5. Like many of the author's works, my ending leaves the reader questioning whether revenge or inaction is the better path.

FINANCES

There's one key difference between state and independent school leadership. State schools undoubtedly face chronic underfunding, but they don't face actual closure due to financial collapse. By contrast, in an independent school, if you cannot balance the books, creditors gather and you close. There is no safety net: students lose their school and everyone loses their job.

For an independent-school proprietor, this creates a unique strain; however glorious your school is, it can still all go wrong if your strategy is wrong and if finances are mismanaged. No wonder venture-capital-backed groups circle constantly overhead. Such groups can offer a lifeline, investing in infrastructure and turning around failing institutions.

FINANCIAL LITERACY

Financial illiteracy is no longer acceptable in a head or in senior leaders. Online courses, YouTube tutorials – there is no excuse. Learn the language of finance. Both head and bursar need an absolute 'ear to the ground' regarding local economics; they also need a financially literate board of governors to challenge assumptions. There's a long roll call of defunct schools out there. Their names linger vaguely in the memory as cautionary tales of strategic misjudgements.

Savvy parents will ask pointed questions about a school's financial health. The first thing any parent working in finance will do is download your accounts from Companies House or the website of The Charity Commission.

CURRENT CRISIS

There's no sugar-coating the reality. Rising operational costs, teacher salary demands, higher national insurance (NI) employer contributions, loss of business rate relief and increased regulatory scrutiny have all added financial strain. Furthermore, with VAT now on school fees, parents face real affordability concerns. The true impact of this likely won't kick in for a year or two, as children reach natural exit points and parents reassess finances. Responsible school leaders must act now.

CUT COSTS, INCREASE REVENUE

There are only two levers to pull: reduce spending or increase income. In reality, you must do both.

For 20 years, the sector has been sleepwalking into a situation where fees rise year on year at a rate far outstripping inflation. Just putting up the fees each year is no longer viable.

THINK CHICKEN FARM

Like their American counterparts, more UK schools need to diversify through auxiliary businesses: summer programmes, conferences, merchandise operations, and so on. All schools must ask, 'What entrepreneurial ventures can we safely embark on to support the school?'

A small charity school I visited in India also owned a chicken farm, with profits directly supporting the school. It's this kind of entrepreneurial thinking all independent schools should consider.

The larger, established schools already run additional business ventures. Leading UK schools have successfully exported their brands internationally – either licensing their names or directly operating satellite schools abroad – generating millions for the coffers of the mother school. Furthermore, they have development officers working tirelessly to secure donations and endowments. But small- and medium-sized schools can also learn from this.

To sum up: all independent schools must now develop diverse revenue streams so that they are not dependent solely on tuition fees.

MANAGING COSTS

Many schools have pulled out of the costly Teachers' Pension Scheme (TPS). It is not reported that these schools are struggling to recruit as a result. For many schools, the TPS is a luxury that needs to be considered carefully in the mid- to long-term.

A fiscally responsible school actively develops budgeting expertise among middle and senior leaders. Effective heads create a culture where seeking value becomes second nature – whether sourcing playground equipment or renegotiating a photocopier lease. After all, better deals can nearly always be found with bargaining. It can and must become an institutional habit, and even a source of fun when a good deal has been achieved.

Consider online or hybrid learning for subjects with small take-up. You may deliver GCSE Latin, for example, more cheaply with an online tutor. Develop antennae that are alert to better possibilities – and always see if you can learn from what other schools are doing.

Teacher salaries (with pension and NI contributions) are your biggest expense. Most schools spend 60–70% of their income on staff. The context of your school will determine the appropriate percentage. Some schools run a tighter ship than this, and much will depend on the nature of your school. Whatever they are, know your figures!

Know what it costs to teach each year group and each subject. Is your early years department losing money? Can you justify another teaching assistant? Is your sixth form more, or less, profitable than your GCSE years?

Understand the costs of convening a meeting in terms of the true cost-per-hour of all staff attending, along with the financial cost of meetings that don't start on time. It certainly focuses minds.

The cost of a teacher is not, of course, just the wage. A salary of £35k is, in reality, more than £45k with NI and pension contributions. But allow also for the Fall Out Factor (FOF) – the true cost of staff whose drama (habitual fall outs with colleagues, parents, pupils) consumes hours of leadership time. Conversely, some staff are worth their weight in gold because they defuse tensions before they escalate. That should be reflected in their salary.

YOUR CATCHMENT AREA

As the sector continues to professionalise, you can be sure that your competitors will be examining catchment and socioeconomic data to inform their strategic planning. It may be a false economy to believe you can do this yourself. Consider professional help to further your understanding of the market.

Keep abreast of new housing developments and infrastructure projects. Identify potential new catchment areas, perhaps with a new bus route to attract families. Transport links are essential. For example, a school in Hampton Court can pick up students from as far away as Vauxhall or Clapham Junction via the Waterloo line.

Don't assume that your educational provision is better than that of nearby state schools. Visit them to understand what you're doing differently. You need clarity on why a parent should give up holidays or home improvements to send their child to your school.

Overseas pupils are an increasingly important revenue source, for day schools and boarding schools alike. Private guardianship arrangements can facilitate the attendance of international students at your school. Consider paying commission to agents to make this happen.

GET THE RIGHT PEOPLE

You have a problem if your finance team lacks expertise. Ask the hard question: do you really have thorough financial expertise *at the heart* of your school? Or do you just have nice people doing their best? If your school is to thrive, hire the best bursar you can afford and upskill key staff.

A full- or part-time development officer might cost a significant salary, but if they oversee fundraising several times that amount (which is generally possible), the return on investment is clear. Moreover, you project an image of a coherent, long-term strategy, which reassures parents.

CASH FLOW IS KING

In some ways, running an independent school is straightforward. You have three main periods where fees come in, and you're paid in advance. The 'term's notice' clause in parent contracts means you can budget more effectively than is possible in many other businesses.

But having terms starting in September, January and April can mean possible cashflow issues, especially over the summer with potentially five months without tuition income. It's a game-changer if you can get some funds in by July rather than September. Consider asking new students to pay in July instead of September. For overseas pupils especially, aim to collect fees by 1st July; it makes a huge cashflow difference and protects against 'no shows'.

PROMPT PAYMENT

You **must** develop a culture where all fees come in by the first day of term. At the end of the first day, the bursar should report on the percentage of fees that have been received. Keep term-by-term comparisons.

Immediately follow up with families with unpaid fees. Sometimes calling one embarrassed parent at home leads to a quicker result than calling the high-flying spouse at work.

Consider offering a 1% discount if fees are paid by the first day of term, or a larger discount if paid a year in advance. A line on the invoice thanking parents for paying by the first day of term can work wonders.

Presentation matters. Parents collecting children at 4pm are taking mental notes. If the grass is overgrown, signage is shabby and classroom furniture damaged, they'll notice. Subconsciously, they'll worry about the school's financial health. Look confident. Look prosperous. Paint the fences.

If everything about your organisation is sharp, the inner compulsion to pay fees on time will be there too.

WHEN FEES AREN'T PAID

You are in a contractual arrangement with parents. If fees aren't paid by half-term, give the family formal notice to remove their child by term's end.

Meeting families in financial distress is painful. But being 'soft' rarely works. Unless you're firm, a parent dealing with multiple problems will put your fees at the bottom of their creditor list.

Remember: if parents owe you £7000, they have a problem. If they owe you £21,000, then *you* have a problem.

Don't make concessions until there's been a forensic examination of their finances. I can cite instances where families given fee remission were later discovered holidaying in Barbados.

STAFF CHILDREN

Fee remission for staff children can help to bind staff to a school. But over time, the cost can be staggering, especially if a staff child takes the place of a full-paying student.

If you give fee remission for staff children, never make a long-term commitment. Reserve the right to review all awards as circumstances change.

IN PUBLIC AND PRIVATE

As a head, publicly you engage in educational debate, connect emotionally with parents and celebrate excellence. You're a wonderful listener, and sometimes you laugh out loud.

But privately, with your financial team, your eye is always on the bottom line.

Independent schools don't collapse because pupils fail exams. They collapse because they run out of money. Running an independent school means leading with vision, but also with nerve and nous and purpose. It means embracing the balance sheet, understanding your costs, diversifying income and always maintaining the illusion of calm prosperity, even when frantically paddling beneath the surface.

This is modern independent school leadership. Adapt, innovate, sharpen your pencil – and paint your fences.

ASIDE
WHO AM I?

1. I was born in the nineteenth century and became one of the most financially successful British writers of my time, known for my sharp observations of human nature.
2. I attended The King's School, Canterbury, where I was bullied for my stammer and my poor English (French had been my first language).
3. I believed that true learning comes not from school but from experience, travel and exposure to different cultures.
4. In one of my novels, the main character rejects formal education and material success in favour of self-discovery through spiritual exploration in India.
5. I am considered a master of the short-story medium, and my work used to feature regularly on the O-level English literature curriculum. Times being what they are, I'm unlikely ever to be a GCSE set text.

GOD

In the first episode of the 1979 BBC documentary *Public School*, Radley College headmaster Dennis Silk addresses new boys in Chapel:

> You may be wondering why I've asked to see you in Chapel. It's a place you'll be spending quite a lot of time in. This school stands for the Christian religion. ... What is important to me is simply this – the *real* religious life begins when you walk out that door. It's how you treat each other.

Silk is explicit that the school is not going to 'coerce' the boys into any particular beliefs, but he is clear about what the school represents. There is calm, there is clarity. The past, as they say, is a foreign country.

Almost half a century later, the spiritual framework in our schools is arguably less clear. Where is spiritual life to be found? Are we explicitly Christian? Are we low-key, enjoying ceremony but downplaying theology? Or are we effectively a pick-and-mix school, as in 'all the religions are great, feel free to choose one, as we don't have a favourite'.

My sister's 1980s school blazer proudly bore the motto 'Serve God and Be Cheerful'. That same school has since replaced it with 'Forging our paths, building the future' – a shift from explicit religious reference to generic aspiration mirroring broader changes in UK society. We increasingly tiptoe around faith lest we offend.

We all agree on educating the mind and exercising the body, but what of the soul? Some non-denominational schools suggest religion is best left to families. Yet childhood is incomplete without exposure to something greater than self, whether through faith, spiritual reflection or a deep sense of wonder. So where does school fit in here?

CHANGING LANDSCAPE

The English public school tradition is historically intertwined with Christianity, and most (though not all) have retained their Latin mottos:

Deo Duce – With God as our leader

Fide et Literis – By faith and learning

Laborare est Orare – To work is to pray

In Fide Vade – Go in faith

Deo Non Fortuna – By God, not by luck

Sancte et Sapienter – With holiness and wisdom

Yet behind these inscriptions, schools have to manage secular expectations while honouring their religious heritage – especially the schools blessed with beautiful chapels. Without our cathedral schools (predominantly independent) and collegiate chapels, our rich musical lineage would likely be lost. Arguably, we gather today primarily to preserve this cultural treasure rather than to serve God. For we kid ourselves if we assume that today's boy and girl choristers are necessarily devout Christians. Bluntly, becoming a chorister has more to do with obtaining a scholarship and financial aid in order to attend the school.

That said, some independent schools boldly and explicitly declare their faith identity, whether it be Muslim, Jewish, Sikh or Christian. Thus, they achieve congruence between stated beliefs and practice, doubtless with the aim of attracting a core of families with shared values. But others struggle with this balance. A growing number of heads, in both the state and independent sectors, are uncertain whether to wish families 'Happy Holidays' or 'Merry Christmas'.

A recent letter to parents from a Hampshire primary school headteacher reads:

> We have decided not to hold the Easter Service this year ... in the spirit of inclusivity and respect for diverse religious beliefs. ... One of the ways we will be celebrating inclusivity is by taking part in Refugee Week.

I don't know the school in question, and this might be the right decision for that community, but the predictable media backlash only serves to highlight how fraught the issue is. However, it is worth considering your own school's position on religion and spiritual matters. It is a useful exercise to see whether or not you can express it in writing (even if you do this only in private).

RELIGIOUS LITERACY

Too often, the national curriculum leaves students ignorant of Judeo-Christian culture. How many pupils understand phrases such as 'the writing on the wall', 'the prodigal son' or 'doubting Thomas'? (Try asking the nearest teenager!) An independent school can take the decision that these things do matter – and proactively weave key cultural reference points into the school's own curriculum. Not for conversion (to which, in any case, there might be resistance), but for cultural and intellectual depth.

MIND, BODY, SOUL

Our education system prioritises mind over body, and body over soul. But without attention to spiritual intelligence – finding meaning in mystery, experiencing wonder, connecting with something greater – we risk producing academically accomplished yet spiritually impoverished students. This, at least, is a value of weekly chapel or indeed any enforced period of silence. It may be the only time your students are tranquil, or have a moment to reflect during the week. It certainly can't do any harm for our anxious generation.

SPIRITUAL INTELLIGENCE

Most leadership qualifications include modules on emotional intelligence and self-awareness. Yet spiritual intelligence – arguably leadership's most profound dimension – rarely features. We can't all be Nelson Mandela, transfigured through our capacity for forgiveness and finding meaning in suffering. But as school leaders, we *can* engage with our deeper spiritual purpose – a world beyond metrics, beyond data, beyond learning outcomes – in order to see the child.

Consider this message from a former pupil:

> One of the most enlightening moments of my childhood was when I was sent to your office crying over an exam paper and you ripped it in half and said 'it doesn't matter'. That moment gave me courage to be myself. It shaped who I have become (I completed my PhD in English last January).

Most teachers will have such stories – of those times when they made a difference to a child's life through a kind of spiritual intuition rather than policy adherence. One advantage independent schools have is their flexibility; the ability occasionally to dispense with a policy when wisdom demands, allowing values rather than rules to govern.

FINDING BALANCE

While working on an education project in India, I visited a school for street children run by the Delhi Brotherhood Society. When I asked its director, Father Amos, why he worked tirelessly for Hindu children without mentioning Christ to them, he stopped his jeep, turned to me and said, 'I never talk about religion'. This was true grace – profound respect for others' beliefs while serving through his own faith. This spiritual dimension – healing and nurturing – need not be proclaimed but must be present.

This offers a model for all school leaders of faith whose beliefs guide their work. Live your values but don't proselytise.

Schools with historic chapels should not shy from using these spaces for reflection, music and community. A skilled chaplain, much like the best *Thought for the Day* contributors on BBC Radio 4, can craft messages that resonate with both believers and non-believers. Even in non-denominational settings, ceremony and tradition hold value. When we introduced a church carol service (lessons and carols format) at my non-religious school, many students experienced their first religious ceremony. And some heard a church organ for the first time too – a valuable cultural education even for non-believers.

A school's recognition of religious traditions should be both sensitive and confident. Wishing 'Merry Christmas' need not be controversial, just as celebrating Diwali should be approached with respect (and genuine understanding) rather than tokenism. For what it's worth, my view is that schools should resist drifting toward anodyne 'Happy Holidays' language that erodes traditions without substantive replacement.

THE SERENITY PRAYER

The Serenity Prayer, attributed to Reinhold Niebuhr, offers wisdom regardless of one's religious beliefs:

> God grant me the serenity to accept the things I cannot change, courage to change the things I can, and wisdom to know the difference.

In Alcoholics Anonymous, members are invited to invoke a 'higher power' – rather than specifically God – if that resonates better with their personal spiritual understanding. For school leaders, this prayer speaks to the essential wisdom of knowing what can and cannot be controlled. A paradox of school leadership is captured in the phrase 'tighten up to be good, loosen to be outstanding'. Finding this balance requires spiritual insight as much as managerial skill.

Perhaps the first thing a new school leader learns is that they cannot control everything. People don't always respond or interact rationally, and learning to 'let go' is a hallmark of effective leadership. What prevents some leaders from achieving serenity – a desirable trait in every headteacher – is their need for absolute control. If faith is not present, then arguably the same strength can come from making time to lean into one's spiritual side.

FINAL THOUGHTS

School leaders seeking to foster spiritual intelligence should:

- create spaces for stillness and reflection
- value ceremony while ensuring inclusivity
- promote religious and cultural literacy across faiths
- model reflective practice in meetings and assemblies
- embody values through daily interactions
- encourage open debates on faith and ethics

- integrate spirituality across disciplines
- recognise that leadership requires moral clarity.

CODA

Whether through traditional faith, humanist values or a broader spirituality, independent school leaders must acknowledge that education is about more than knowledge acquisition or career preparation. It is about shaping whole beings – mind, body and soul – equipped to lead lives of meaning, purpose and service.

An independent school that neglects the spiritual dimension of education becomes little more than a financially advantaged test-taking centre. The world's finest schools, be they secular or faith-based, understand that education is about the *whole person*. They cultivate intellectual curiosity, physical discipline and – crucially – a sense of something greater than oneself.

In our materialistic, distracted world, spiritually intelligent leadership may be our greatest gift to the next generation. It reminds us that what matters most is not what we know or what we have, but who we are.

ASIDE

WHO AM I?

1. My early career was in teaching and school leadership, and I became the Headmaster of Repton School at the young age of 27.
2. It is alleged by Roald Dahl in his autobiography *Boy* that I personally administered severe beatings to boys under my care.
3. I later pursued a career in the Church of England, eventually rising to become Archbishop of Canterbury.
4. In 1948, I christened the future King Charles III in the music room at Buckingham Palace.
5. In 1953, I presided over the coronation of Queen Elizabeth II, and placed the crown on her head in front of the world's television cameras.

HEART

Leadership in an independent school is often evaluated by the governors (or the proprietor) through strategic acumen, academic results and financial sustainability. Yet beneath these indicators, there's a less tangible but arguably more essential quality – *heart*. This chapter proposes that heart is by no means a sentimental metaphor but an organising principle of ethical, pastoral and even intellectual leadership.

HEART AS COURAGE

The Latin *cor* gives us both 'heart' and 'courage'. It is not a coincidence. The best educators demonstrate a brave compassion – an ability to feel for, and sometimes suffer with, their students.

It's evident in extreme moments, such as when staff members scurry around at 5pm at no notice, working out how they can house three small children in order to stop them going into local authority care. Or the moment a teacher gently takes the car key away from a parent who's clearly intoxicated, managing the situation sensitively so not to distress the child.

This courage-of-the-heart is also literal: the 21-year-old Wolverhampton nursery teacher Lisa Potts shielding the children in her care from a crazed machete attack; or Philip Lawrence, headmaster of St George's in Maida Vale, London, who was stabbed to death outside his school when he intervened to protect one of his students who was being attacked by a gang. These cases haunt the educational profession because they illustrate the extreme end of a spectrum we all inhabit. At some level, all teachers *would* put themselves between a child and danger. Why?

Because teaching is not transactional. It is vocational. And at the centre of vocation is love.

LEADING WITH AFFECTION

Imagine the first assembly of term in an all-through school: three-year-olds sitting cross-legged at your feet, looking up at you with huge saucer eyes, while sixth formers lounge in the shadows at the back. You stand before them not merely as a figure of authority, but as the moral centre of the school. What do you feel?

If you do not feel a wave of affection – if you do not feel stirred by the sight of this sea of unformed humanity, some of whom will become poets, some addicts, some parents, some broken – you are not ready to lead. A school head must emanate *affection*, even *tenderness*, for the children and teenagers in their care.

PASTORAL IMAGINATION

The heart of the school is not found in its policies but in its people.

Where is the heart of your school? Watch for those daily moments that reveal it. With the little ones, are teachers helping them with coats just efficiently – or are they doing it gently, with love and eye contact? Does someone notice when a normally buoyant teenager falls silent and quietly check in with them after class?

Fifty years on, as I write this, I can still feel the arm of the art teacher who put her arm round me, as I was crying in my first ever Latin exam. 'It's all right,' she whispered to me, 'I want you to know, I can't do the questions either'.

FRAGILE HEARTS

Let us never forget the hidden vulnerabilities within our schools.

Students may appear polished, articulate and resilient, or even rude sometimes, but behind the façade, some are anxious, traumatised or insecure. The chances are that at least a handful of your students are dealing silently with pains and pressures of which you are unaware.

It is as well to remember that when your eyes scan the year groups in assembly.

Staff (both teaching and non-teaching staff) are vulnerable too. The emotional demands of pastoral care can be immense. Checking in with staff, especially those you know to be dealing with challenging situations, is a must. Ideally all staff are looking out for each other. It's a valuable safety net if you've missed something and a member of staff comes to you to say, 'I'm a bit worried about so-and-so'.

LEADING WITH HEART

Organisational leadership is in many ways a science, and there's a huge amount to be gleaned from existing literature, from McKinsey frameworks to SWOT analysis, from Belbin team roles to anything written by the late Charles Handy. But more is needed. Leadership development transcends mere skill acquisition. It centres on personal transformation as a continuing journey. In this sense, meaningful personal growth enhances our leadership capabilities. When we, as school leaders, really work on our emotional intelligence – developing empathy, humility and moral clarity – our greater influence and presence are felt by all.

As educational leaders, we must stress the joy and beauty to be found in life; we are after all robustly optimistic by nature. But life can be brutal. And each of us carries personal pain, however neatly compartmentalised. Our individual ways of processing loss, failure, injustice or betrayal will shape our leadership, because although we may be hurt, we're still standing. Yes, we may keep our pain private, but these experiences ultimately strengthen our leadership, deepening our capacity to form authentic heart-to-heart connections with students, staff and parents alike.

Heart-led schools are instantly recognisable. They are animated by warmth rather than efficiency. Relationships always take precedence over outcomes. There is space for beauty and paradox – and mistakes. Children feel seen. Staff feel trusted. Parents feel heard.

HEART AS JOY

With mental-health fragility such an issue these days – among students, staff and, indeed, heads themselves – protecting joy is a core responsibility. Sometimes this means allowing a magical learning moment to extend beyond the bell, or laughing at ourselves when a lesson goes awry. The head should be, in effect, the *guardian of joy*, while simultaneously managing the serious matters that inevitably arise each week. Our challenge is to absorb these pressures without appearing burdened; finding ways to shoulder responsibilities while maintaining a positive presence.

Do students smile at you and acknowledge you when they walk by? Are children eager to reach their next lesson, excited by what awaits them? Do parents leave open days moved to tears by words that touched their hearts? Does your school *sing* – both metaphorically and literally?

Ask yourself honestly: when your name is mentioned in staffroom conversations or playground chatter, is it associated with joy?

HEART AND AI

Teachers are fast getting to grips with how AI can help lighten their workload – generating lesson plans, creating tests, summarising study materials – and students seem perfectly at ease learning digitally, with marked work returned via platforms, with some assessments handled by AI. The way we learn, and perhaps even how we define knowledge itself, is on the move.

Independent schools, with their freedom to innovate, are already pioneering a number of developments. Adaptive assessments, for instance, have quickly become standard for 11+ testing. And learning in future will doubtless be customised by these systems, helping students progress at a pace and in a style that suits their individual needs. That's all to the good.

Yet if this chapter – and perhaps this entire book – repeatedly returns to concepts like heart and love, it's deliberate. We need a counterbalance. As schools embrace greater automation and systematic approaches, we must strive to value and preserve imperfection and the human element.

We've already witnessed how readily education can drift into a world of jargon, data points and progress charts. We seem hesitant to affirm that education extends far beyond measuring progress in a few narrow areas.

More than ever, we need to help young people become themselves. Schools must fundamentally reconsider their approach, with independent schools potentially better positioned to lead this transformation due to their greater autonomy. We need to prioritise relationships, laughter and kindness above all else.

And while AI might help us teach more efficiently, it should never be allowed to make us forget why we're teaching in the first place.

CHECKLIST

- **Are you considered kind?** Would students, staff and parents associate your leadership with joy, warmth and humanity?
- **Do you prioritise people over process?** When in doubt, do you choose relationships over efficiency?
- **Is emotional intelligence a criterion for promotion?** Do you place a particular value on staff who are emotionally astute, or do you primarily reward those who deliver measurable outputs and results?
- **Do you actively protect joy?** Have you created deliberate spaces in the timetable and curriculum for humour, creativity, surprise and wonder?
- **Have you safeguarded the wellbeing of the staff?** Can you identify which teachers might be quietly burning out? What systems support their emotional health?
- **Do you allow for vulnerability?** Do you allow for failure, gentleness and authentic connection across our community?
- **What kind of hearts are you helping pupils grow?** Are you forming not only capable minds but also generous, compassionate souls?

ASIDE

WHO AM I?

1. I was heavily influenced by progressive educational thinkers, including psychoanalysts like Freud and Wilhelm Reich, who emphasised emotional wellbeing in learning.
2. In the 1920s, I founded my own school in Suffolk, which became one of the most famous alternative schools in the world.
3. At my school, students were given freedom to choose what, when and how they learned – there were no compulsory lessons.
4. My school continues to operate today, embodying my belief in child-led education and personal freedom.
5. I wrote extensively on my educational philosophy, with my most famous book simply titled *Summerhill*, which remains a key text in alternative education.

INEQUALITY

We have a global reputation for world-class education and the UK enjoys considerable soft power as a result – not just in terms of our leading universities but our independent day and boarding schools too. Data from Jisc indicates that the UK has educated 50 world leaders – more national leaders than any other country in the world. This is a time to be proud of our reputation and achievement.

Meanwhile, each year teachers move between the sectors, from the state to the independent and vice versa. Moreover, many independent-school heads were educated in the state sector and a number of state-school heads were educated in the private sector. And up and down the country there are fruitful and meaningful partnerships between schools from both sectors who are determined to make a difference to the communities they serve. And, indeed, we should all be in this together.

Contributing to and sharing with the wider local community is an essential part of leadership today in all our independent schools. Furthermore, independent schools support the state sector by offering teacher-training opportunities, providing access to music and the arts, and – perhaps most of all – supporting and transforming the lives of children and teenagers with special educational needs and disabilities (SEND) who may struggle in mainstream schools.

The vision must be for the two sectors to work together – supporting each other, learning from each other – for the benefit of all young people. The School Partnerships Alliance website is essential reading for everyone who works in education; it is a testament to the imaginative and impactful work that is taking place right now all over the country.

It is a vision of optimism and a resolute desire to work together for the betterment of all.

Yet the public narrative on independent schools stubbornly refuses to shift. We can all do more to forge connections and to influence public perception, for the tedious media narrative continues to bang on about inequality and the privileged 6–7% in the independent-school system. As we know, students move between the sectors, as do teachers. Over a third of all pupils in Independent Schools Council (ISC) schools receive financial assistance, and many thousands attend independent schools without paying anything. There are countless stories of lives transformed by the sector.

Oxbridge is often cited as an example of academic success, but it's as well to remember that each year a good number of students who achieve Oxbridge places come from the independent sector on bursaries, and sometimes full bursaries. To the best of its abilities, the sector is playing a significant role in facilitating social mobility and is constantly exploring what more it can do. But, of course, the narrative rarely, if ever, conveys this.

Furthermore, plenty of students leave independent education at 16+ (for financial reasons) to take their A-levels at one of the many excellent state sixth-form colleges. Conversely, many leave their state school (their families having put money aside over the years) to take A-levels at an independent sixth form. It is thus not always clear what is meant by 'a state-school pupil' in government data.

Let's acknowledge a few things that don't always get said aloud. Many schools in the sector are financially fragile, working on tight margins, and serving a community. Half of all ISC independent schools have fewer than 290 pupils, and one-quarter have under 155 pupils. They rely on careful budgeting and often stretch themselves to offer bursaries and financial assistance. They really are doing their best!

We should also celebrate the specialisms that independent schools offer: music, dance, sport, special-needs provision, boarding, single-sex education or international qualifications like the International Baccalaureate (IB). These schools fill important gaps in the national educational landscape and, in many cases, they compensate for what the state system is unable – or unwilling – to provide. All the finalists in the BBC Young Musician of Year competition in 2024 came from the independent sector. If this is an example of inequality, this is not the independent sector's fault. The question is: why isn't the government doing more to support music provision and the arts in the state sector?

Meanwhile, most state schools are stretched to breaking point. They are woefully underfunded, and pastoral support is buckling under the strain of rising mental-health issues. Then we have the seemingly silent scandal: the so-called 'forgotten third' – those students who leave school without basic qualifications in English and maths. Why aren't we screaming? It's this that should be filling our airwaves. This is the inequality we should all be focusing on.

JOHN RAWLS'S THOUGHT EXPERIMENT

If we were designing a national education system from scratch – and we didn't know in advance whether we'd be rich or poor, north or south, white or black, male or female – what kind of system would we create?

The American philosopher John Rawls, in his magnum opus *A Theory of Justice* (1971), called this the 'veil of ignorance'. His challenge was simple: build a just society, assuming you might be born anywhere in it. You might end up in Tower Hamlets or Tunbridge Wells, in a refugee family or a middle-class home with books on every shelf.

Would we, behind that veil, be satisfied with the society we currently have? Probably not.

What we might want – behind that veil – is a system where the state sector is so well-funded, so inspiring, so rich in opportunity, that families with money no longer feel the need to seek something different. This should be our national objective. It will take real political will, cross-party consensus, long-term thinking and a significant reinvestment in our schools; perhaps a full 2% of GDP more than we currently spend.

MAKING A POSITIVE CASE

Meanwhile, independent school leaders today must be prepared to advocate positively and proactively for the benefits of a private sector in the national ecosystem. We could be a lean, standard-setting sector that contributes to the regeneration of the whole school system by taking an inspirational lead across a range of good practice (diversity and inclusion, curriculum reform, implementation of AI, and so on).

All independent school leaders have a part to play in this story. This means reading widely, studying carefully reports on inequality in education as they come out from the Institute for Fiscal Studies (IFS), the Private Education Policy Forum (PEPF) and other think-tanks – and we need to be prepared to engage with the findings.

The same goes for all state school leaders, for there's wisdom and good practice in the independent sector. Dismissing it all as elitist or outdated misses opportunities for mutual learning. The best leadership – in either sector – demonstrates sufficient humility to say, 'I don't have all the answers, but I want to be part of the conversation.'

So, what do we do with all this? We embrace the tension. We recognise the complexity. We stop pretending that the debate is simple. And, above all, we try to move beyond slogans and soundbites into something more intelligent, more generous and more hopeful.

SUGGESTED STEPS FOR SCHOOL LEADERS

- **Read both sides of the current political argument**. Engage with challenging reports (e.g. IFS, PEPF) as well as defences of the sector.
- **Build partnerships**. Joint events, staff exchanges, shared CPD – collaboration and mutual understanding beat competition.
- **Visit state schools**. Understand what they do well and what their challenges are.
- **Widen your bursary provision**. Make this a priority and part of your purpose.
- **Acknowledge complexity**. Avoid sweeping claims and defensiveness. Invite discussion.
- **Celebrate excellence in all schools**. Don't assume that your way is the only, or the best, way.
- **Help your students understand inequality**. Let them see the broader picture and build empathy, civic awareness and responsibility.

- **Support national reinvestment in education.** Use your voice to call for improved state funding.

In the end, perhaps our best contribution – as educators – is to model what it means to think deeply, argue respectfully and keep asking the right questions. Not because we have to, but because, behind the veil of ignorance, we would want others to do the same.

ASIDE
WHAT PLAY AM I?

1. I am a British play first performed in 1968, written by one of the writers of the Beyond the Fringe stage revue.
2. My setting is a fictional English public school called Albion House, where students and staff gather for an end-of-year performance.
3. Through satire and humour, I critique the fading influence of the British Empire and question the role of elite education in shaping the nation's leaders.
4. The headmaster, played by John Gielgud in the original production, represents the old guard; someone who sees the school's traditions as vital but also struggles to defend them.
5. My title, which takes its name from the Harrow School song, suggests the passage of time and nostalgia, yet my message warns against uncritical reverence for the past.

JUGGLING

I was just doing it, you stupid woman. I just put it down, to come here and be reminded by you to do what I'm already doin'. I mean, what is the point in reminding me to do what I'm already doing? I mean, what is the bloody point? I'm doing it, aren't I? Yes, yes, I picked it up. ... Yes ... No, no, I haven't had a chance yet. ... I've been at it solidly ever since I got back. Yes, I will. ... Yes ... No, I haven't yet, but I will. ... Yes, yes, yes, I know it is. ... Yes, I'll try and get it cleared up. ... Anything else? I mean, would you like the hotel moved a bit to the left?

Basil Fawlty, *Fawlty Towers* (1975)

Between demanding jobs, personal worries, health concerns and the constant ping of digital notifications, it's no wonder so many of us feel overworked and under-slept. The line between work and home has all but vanished; tiredness, stress and burnout have become normalised. And it's not just we who feel the strain – our relationships take a hit too. When you're mentally exhausted, it's hard to be truly present for the people you love.

In school leadership, the pressure intensifies even further. You're not just juggling tasks and numerous commitments; you're holding together an entire community, sometimes making tough decisions with profound consequences for others. Students, staff, parents, policies, results – it all lands on your shoulders.

YOU NEED A SYSTEM

The job can't be done without a trusted system to manage your workflow and myriad commitments. Years ago, a desk diary and to-do list might have sufficed, but that's not enough to lead today's complex schools.

Take a moment to evaluate how you're coping with your life, especially if it's been a while since your last assessment. Consider the array of business books, productivity guides and time-management apps available – all designed to help optimise your thinking and workflow. Whatever system you currently use, it's worth asking yourself, 'Could there be a better way to manage my life?'.

Speak to others whose efficiency and effectiveness you admire. What principles do they apply to their lives? Without continual effort to refine your systems for handling information and workflow, you'll find yourself in a Sisyphean struggle – endlessly pushing the boulder uphill without making meaningful progress.

The two systems that have served me best also complement each other. They are:

1. Stephen Covey's *The 7 Habits of Highly Effective People* (1989). This book offers timeless principles of self-management. Working through all seven habits takes time and serious reflection. But new habits will eventually become part of you.
2. David Allen's *Getting Things Done* (2015). Allen provides a comprehensive approach to managing everything in your life. You can grasp the principles quickly with one read-through, but mastering them takes time. There's an active community of GTD practitioners, and connecting with them online or in real life is an excellent way to meet high-performing professionals outside education.

A key principle of GTD is the adoption of a ruthless system for handling all incoming items:

- delegate it
- incubate it – fix a time when you'll address it
- do it immediately
- discard it.

> Your mind is for having ideas, not holding them.
>
> David Allen.

Allen speaks of achieving 'a mind like water' when you've off-loaded all your commitments and thoughts into a trusted system, so that your brain isn't spinning, trying to remember, or juggle, them.

Without the overview of all your tasks that GTD provides, you can never know whether you're focusing on your most important tasks. As Peter Drucker said in his 1966 book *The Effective Executive*, 'Efficiency is doing things right. Effectiveness is doing the right things.'

THREE PRINCIPLES FOR SUCCESSFUL JUGGLING

1. Master self-management

Define your unshakeable principles and deeper purpose. Write down your mission statement and review it periodically. As a leader, you'll want to be seen as congruent, with your decisions, actions and beliefs aligned.

Become a master of managing workflow so you aren't stressed by competing demands. You cannot rest properly or sleep if your mind is churning with unfinished tasks. To be a master juggler, put in the hours of thinking that will ultimately help you become a more efficient leader. Consider taking a long weekend to do deep thinking and work through productivity systems.

You need to master time management – or rather, self-management – since you can't manage time itself.

In essence: don't even think of managing others if you aren't managing yourself.

2. Prioritise harmony at home

You can't juggle if your mind is distracted and your heart is in turmoil. This is a tough one because most of us will have challenging periods in our lives. One of the most debilitating pains is having an unhappy home life or being in a toxic relationship.

My urgent message: if you're considering senior leadership or headship, don't do it if your personal life is a shambles. Somehow you need to sort out your personal life first, whether that's your marriage or current relationship. You simply cannot be the leader your school deserves if your home life is wretched.

3. Make self-care non-negotiable

Focus on yourself first. You have numerous balls in the air, but self-care must be a priority. This means making time for activities you enjoy, whether golf, guitar or gardening. It means being careful – even fastidious – with your diet and physical health.

This may not be very politically correct, but if you look unhealthy and unfit, you're signalling to the world that you're not managing well. We expect our students to make the best of themselves; as a school leader, you need to lead in this area too. Consider your image carefully.

Think of this as a pyramid:

1. **Choose systems that work for you** – consciously work to become better at time management.
2. **Prioritise a harmonious home life** – exit from toxic relationships.
3. **Prioritise your wellbeing** – including fitness, diet and appearance.

You will occasionally fall off the wagon, which is fine. Everyone does. The key is to notice and recover. Sometimes life happens, and that's okay.

Self-care isn't a luxury – it's essential. Without it, the whole system starts to buckle. We can't look after others if we're not looking after ourselves.

Stress is real and potentially deadly. Ask a trusted colleague whether you appear generally relaxed, or noticeably stressed. You need people around you to tell you the truth. Get help if needed. In extreme cases, have the self-awareness to step back and take time off.

THE IN-TRAY EXERCISE

Try this exercise, designed for deputy-head interviews.

Imagine you are the deputy head of an all-through school. Take a pencil and quickly write 1 to 7 in the margin below, indicating your priority order for addressing these issues. Do it quickly. Don't overthink.

It is 8am. You're scheduled to observe a lesson (period 1, 8.50am), teach periods 2 and 3, and meet with a teacher in period 4. You want to keep the afternoon free for a 4pm presentation that requires you to leave by 3pm.

- The receptionist has informed you that she has had a particularly angry and aggressive parent on the phone demanding an appointment with you. The receptionist indicated that you are not available until lunchtime. The parent became abusive to the receptionist and shouted that they are 'on their way to the school now to sort this out'. You have no idea what this is about.
- A teacher has emailed and is very upset about the lesson feedback they were given by the Head of Department in a lesson observation yesterday. They want to speak to you about it urgently.
- A pupil has had an accident at the school gates and needs taking to A&E.
- A parent has emailed to say that they will be collecting their child at lunchtime because she is unwell and doesn't want to do sport.
- Another parent has emailed to say that her daughter has a music lesson scheduled today but this is in the middle of her maths test.
- The registrar has sent you an email about an issue that needs further investigation: a member of staff has made inappropriate comments to a student in a lesson.
- The headmaster has just sent you a text message saying he is detained and is asking if you can take the morning assembly at 8.35am.

I trust you are not reading this and thinking this sounds like a usual day. But days like this certainly can happen from time to time, even in the best-run schools. There might be some differences in opinion about a couple of the items, but broadly speaking the correct sequence would be:

1. **A pupil needs to go to A&E** – the safeguarding emergency takes precedence
    - ensure first aid; delegate to a trusted colleague
    - inform parents immediately
    - follow up with parents in the evening

2. **Angry parent en route** – safety issue
   - alert senior staff and security
   - arrange for a skilled colleague to assist with de-escalation
   - support the receptionist
3. **Morning assembly request** – imminent operational need
   - reply confirming yes
   - prepare briefly; appear calm and in control
   - brief headmaster later
4. **Inappropriate staff comments** – serious safeguarding concern but not urgent
   - acknowledge message and confirm later meeting
   - inform designated safeguarding lead (DSL) and headmaster
   - begin documentation process
5. **Teacher upset after lesson feedback** – staff morale issue
   - acknowledge email, promising to address concerns
   - schedule conversation for later
   - listen and mediate as needed
6. **Music lesson vs test clash** – timetabling issue
   - delegate to appropriate administrator
   - ensure communication with parent and pupil
   - review relevant policies
7. **Unwell student** – routine notification
   - forward to relevant departments
   - ensure proper recording in systems

GENERAL PRINCIPLES

- Stay calm.
- Delegate where possible.
- Maintain communication.

- Document incidents.
- Reflect on systemic improvements.

See the big picture

You need to be able to handle immediate pressures while simultaneously maintaining perspective. You need to consciously shift between modes: 'right now I'm managing day-to-day events and competing priorities' and 'now I'm in mid- to long-term planning mode'. Always be conscious of which mode you are in. Even making time for these two perspectives is itself a juggling act.

Manage relationships

Independent school leadership involves managing relationships between governors/proprietors, staff, parents and pupils. You are the conduit through which everything runs.

Anything that involves 'managing a relationship' needs to be prioritised in your mind.

Social media and the school's online presence also require management and oversight as part of reputation maintenance. Don't entirely delegate this to others. Search up the name of your school routinely online to see what comes up.

Know when to drop balls

Juggling is a precarious activity, but sometimes you need to drop a ball (or let a plate crash) as a conscious decision. Sometimes this is the least-bad decision when in a challenging situation with rising emotions and competing pulls on your time and attention.

In particular, learn to recognise those danger periods when high stress from one incident can lead you to mishandle the next. You may need to step back for a moment before dealing straight away with the next issue. It's the 'straw that broke the camel's back' scenario, so maintain conscious awareness – at all times – of where you are on the stress-threshold continuum.

Trust in your team

Trust is key in developing effective leadership teams. Sometimes juggling means catching each other's balls; delegating, supporting and collaborating to manage the complex demands of school leadership.

Look out for each other – just as surgical teams who have worked together for years anticipate each other's needs, passing instruments before they're verbally requested. In a similar way, you are building a team where you can exchange a glance and know when to step in and support another colleague with a challenging student. Take stock and consider to what extent you have this kind of teamwork in place. If you do not, think consciously about the steps you might need to take.

KEY TAKEAWAYS FOR EFFECTIVE JUGGLING

- **Build robust systems**: make time to develop workflow and information management systems that work for you. Review and refine them regularly.
- **Master yourself before leading others**: self-management is the foundation of effective leadership. You cannot lead a school if you cannot lead yourself.
- **Ensure home harmony**: a turbulent personal life will undermine your professional effectiveness. Address relationship issues before taking on leadership positions.
- **Prioritise your wellbeing**: your physical and mental health are non-negotiable. Model the self-care you want your school community to practise.
- **Practise triage**: develop a keen sense of what's truly urgent and important, as opposed to what is just important, and what can wait or be delegated.
- **Maintain perspective**: regularly zoom out from daily operations to consider long-term vision and strategy.
- **Build a trusted team**: surround yourself with capable people who complement your skills (indeed where you know each other's strengths and weaknesses); people that can be trusted to 'catch balls' when necessary.

- **Know your limits**: recognise when to say no, when to drop certain responsibilities and when to ask for help.

Effective juggling in school leadership isn't about keeping everything perfectly in the air all the time. It's about making conscious choices about what deserves your attention now, what can wait and what can be handled by others.

The best jugglers know that the secret isn't superhuman dexterity – it's the wisdom to know which balls to keep in motion and which to set aside.

ASIDE

WHO AM I?

1. I am a fictional English teacher at an elite all-boys boarding school, where tradition and discipline dominate the culture.
2. Instead of relying on rote learning, I use unconventional methods, such as having students stand on desks to gain new perspectives.
3. My love for poetry includes admiration for Walt Whitman, whose verses I use to inspire my students.
4. One of my students, deeply moved by my lessons, pursues his passion for acting despite his strict father's wishes – with tragic consequences.
5. Even after being forced to leave, my influence on my students endures, culminating in a final, emotional display of loyalty and respect.

KINDERGARTEN

In Germany, children are kinder.

Anon

One of the joys of running a K12 (all-through) school is seeing up close life's journey from kindergarten to young adulthood. This was brought vividly home one afternoon when, as a new head, I was signing off the school's potty-training policy. I may have started my career teaching A-level and international O-level English (back in the day), but more and more, I find myself drawn to the core value and importance of early years.

For any secondary school teacher, I urge you, if you haven't already read it, to download and read the Early Years Foundation Stage (EYFS) statutory framework (Department for Education, 2014). It has undergone a number of revisions, but today is a robust and meaningful document that applies to all early years providers in England and covers children from birth to 5 years old.

The framework covers seven areas of learning:

- Communication and language
- Physical development
- Personal, social and emotional development
- Literacy
- Mathematics
- Understanding the world
- Expressive arts and design

So important is the EYFS that its implementation is mandatory for all childcare providers on the early years register, including maintained and non-maintained schools, independent schools, private nurseries and childminders.

It is the nearest we have to a universal approach to education (used in around 70,000 settings in England). It means that you can convene early years practitioners from very different settings and yet they share a common language. The EYFS came out of the 'Every Child Matters' legislation (Gov.uk, 2003) and is a sound and sensible framework. Over almost two decades, the EYFS has played a key role in raising standards and reducing disparities. It is a highly 'professionalised' area of education, and those who work in early years quite rightly take pride in their qualifications.

BEYOND THE FRAMEWORK

But let me throw in a caveat. Just because someone has an early years qualification, knows the EYFS framework back to front, and can talk fluently in educational jargon doesn't necessarily mean that they're especially attuned to the emotional and developmental needs of very young children.

For quite a few years – though thankfully it has eased a little now – there was a heavy emphasis on assessment and documentation. Practitioners were constantly having to observe, record and interpret what children were doing, especially when it came to child-initiated learning. Sometimes they were expected to read an awful lot into very little: if a child asked whether it was still raining, this might end up being logged as evidence of their understanding of the natural world. It all became a bit tick-box at times. What is more, with no national system in place to check whether different practitioners were interpreting things the same way, the data collected – though often well-intentioned – was largely subjective. That made it tricky to rely on when looking at broader trends across the country.

In other cases, the whole thing tipped over into the frankly absurd. Pupils who could read perfectly well for their age could be marked down in assessments because a reception teacher might have been told that unless a child *chose* to go to the book corner *unprompted*, read out loud to themselves at just the right level, *and* made thoughtful comments about what they'd read – all entirely spontaneously – they couldn't be said to have met the expected standard. Naturally, some teachers ended up playing the game: inventing a bit of creative fiction to satisfy what they saw as a ridiculous system built on hoops rather than sense.

Worse, there is the risk that when a teacher becomes so focused on being the model 'professional', keeping every bit of paperwork immaculate (thus satisfying Ofsted to get the 'outstanding' rating) by being a 'professional teacher', they end up missing daily opportunities to stretch and truly engage the pupils in front of them.

HEART-LED TEACHING

When it comes to appointing staff in early years, the key is this: you need someone with love in their heart, aligned with a deep-seated interest and curiosity in how very young children learn. Someone who is intrigued by how language develops, who reads widely on the subject and who is curious about how differently other countries approach early education – places like Scandinavia or parts of Asia. That kind of fascination really ought to come first. The EYFS framework, the qualifications, the training – all important, of course – should come *after* that instinctive drive to understand how small children make sense of the world. Not before.

There is also an ongoing, and still unresolved, tension between many heart-led early years practitioners – who cherish seeing their pupils play, laugh, explore the world and fall in love with stories – and the government's continued insistence on compulsory baseline testing in literacy and numeracy. In particular, there's pressure for reception-aged pupils to be pushed harder in reading and maths, often at the expense of the very experiences that make early learning rich, joyful and developmentally sound.

THE INEQUALITY GAP

And yet, there really *is* a national problem. Some children (and socio-economic factors play a role here) are arriving at school not yet toilet trained, with limited language skills, underdeveloped social skills and far too much screen time. At the other end of the spectrum, some children come from homes where there has been serious investment – financial, yes perhaps, but mainly emotional and intellectual. Some of these children have been read to daily, since the day they were born. They may have a Spanish-speaking or even Mandarin-speaking nanny (very in vogue a few years ago). They might already be doing ballet, learning the violin and piano, and chatting confidently with adults.

The difference between a child of four who has had that kind of early investment and one who hasn't is heartrending. The gap in neurological sophistication, communication, attention and social ease is staggering. A child who starts off so far behind at four is, statistically, likely to still be behind – significantly so – by the time they reach secondary school. The playing field isn't just uneven for some; it's tilted from the very beginning.

RESPECTING EARLY YEARS STAFF

And this is where we all have a part to play. Those of us working in secondary education can sometimes fall into the trap of thinking that the high-level work we do – teaching quantum mechanics or guiding students through long-run aggregate supply curves – is where the real intellectual heavy lifting happens. And yes, it *is* demanding, and working with teenagers can certainly be challenging. But across the country, early years teachers are too often overlooked; their work quietly underestimated. If you are teaching A-level and want to know what real stamina looks like, try spending an afternoon in a reception classroom.

We in education need to get better at bowing our heads – yes, even genuflecting a little – in respect to those who teach at the very start of the journey. All of us make mistakes with students now and then. With older ones, we can explain ourselves, apologise, repair. But with the youngest children, one thoughtless comment, one careless tone of voice, can do lasting damage. You can shut a child down without even realising it.

The work of nurturing and guiding these small, still-forming human beings is nothing short of transformative – though the effects may not be visible for years. The kind of early years schooling children have could even influence whether or not they are able to go on to form trust-filled romantic relationships in their life. These early years are when a child builds their internal working model of the world – the emotional blueprint for how relationships work and whether the world is a safe, responsive place.

So, if you work in early years, never doubt it: you are building brains, day in, day out. And the rest of us should honour that work.

THE CRITICAL FIRST YEARS

Viewers of Michael Apted's *Seven Up!* documentary series (1964–now) will recognise this line (an old Jesuit saying) – and the haunting insight it contains.

Give me the child until he is seven, and I will give you the man.

Foundations are laid early. Patterns of attachment, confidence, language and trust are being shaped in those fragile, exuberant, astonishingly formative years.

SOME GENTLE REMINDERS

So here are a few gentle reminders for us all – whether we're directly involved in early years or not:

- Take small children seriously when they speak to you. Put down your device, make eye contact and show interest.
- Avoid the temptation to speak in over-simplified, sing-song 'baby talk'. Small children thrive on a rich vocabulary. Let's speak to them as whole people.
- Create space for wonder and curiosity. Answer their questions honestly, even the difficult ones, using age-appropriate language but don't shy away from truth.
- When choosing storybooks, aim just above the child's current level. It's for us to provide the scaffolding and explain the odd word as we go along. Choose stories with depth; narratives with emotional truth, beauty, complexity and nuance.
- Embrace the outdoors and unstructured play. Try not to interrupt children when they are in full-flow and playing imaginatively.

- Our first role, with all small children, is to give confidence – to help a child believe that their voice matters, that they deserve to be heard and that they have full value.

EXEMPLARY PRACTICE

One dance teacher I knew exemplified this beautifully: she taught ballet to teenagers, entered them for exams, choreographed major performances – but her dedication to the youngest children was no less profound.

She made costumes for nursery and reception pupils, and always included them 'with the big children' in the end-of-term show. They were integral. The littlest ones watched the older students with wonder, and then came their moment: on stage, to gasps and applause. One year, a reception child forgot her place mid-dance and 'froze'. Unprompted, an older girl slipped onto the stage, took her hand and gently guided her back into position – graceful, unflustered. It was a small moment. But in truth, it was *everything*.

There is no national framework that can capture this kind of culture. It happens when you build a spirit-filled team of loving, emotionally intelligent educators; those who understand, instinctively, that very young children are not lesser beings, but simply less-experienced ones. Their thoughts, fears, hopes, ideas and feelings are as valid as those of any adult – perhaps more so for being unfiltered and unguarded. And anyone who has seen a five-year-old child seamlessly speak three languages – French with their mother, Spanish with their father, English at school – will know just how utterly extraordinary young minds can be.

A CALL TO SCHOOL LEADERS

And to school leaders – whether in prep schools or all-through schools – make time to visit your early years classrooms. Do it with intention. Bring something to share – a puppet, a toy, an interesting object – and be ready to sit on a small chair and read a story. Your presence matters, signalling that this is the very heart of the school.

And, just as importantly, let your wider staff know how deeply you value your early years colleagues. Speak of them with the honour they deserve. Esteem, after all, is contagious.

Just the other day, I noticed this sign for an all-through school in north-west London, which has just lowered its starting age from three to two:

> Your through-school journey of
> exploration and wonder now starts at 2+

That seems to me to strike exactly the right note.

ASIDE

WHO AM I?

1. I was born in Italy in the nineteenth century, at a time when women had few opportunities in higher education.
2. In 1907, I opened my first educational institution, known as Casa dei Bambini (Children's House).
3. My method emphasised practical life skills, sensory-based learning and freedom within structure.
4. I designed specialised learning materials – such as sandpaper letters and movable alphabets – to help children develop literacy and numeracy.
5. Despite facing political challenges, including exile during World War II, my legacy in education remains profound and influential.

LATIN

EXISTENTIAL CRISIS

The ability to decline and conjugate in Latin was once a rite of passage for pupils (mainly boys) in Britain's preparatory and grammar schools. Textbooks such as Kennedy's *Shorter Latin Primer* (1962), with their densely packed pages of declensions and conjugations, presented Latin as an intricate code. But Latin was more than just a subject – it was a symbol of intellectual rigour, arguably a tool for social mobility and a cornerstone of a classical education.

However, Latin now finds itself at a crossroads, facing an existential crisis, owing to the rise of new subjects and a decline in the number of Latin teachers. This chapter will argue that the future of Latin, and to some extent classical education itself, rests precariously in the realm of the independent sector. A British Council survey in 2020 revealed that Latin is taught at key stage 3 (KS3) in a mere 2.7% of state schools, compared to 49% of independent schools.

The state-sector figure is likely much lower today, given the recent axing of the Latin Excellence Programme – a cost-saving exercise astonishingly implemented mid-year. True, Latin can appear quaint, irrelevant and, at worst, elitist (admittedly not helped by Jacob Rees-Mogg and Boris Johnson deliberately quoting Latin in order to obfuscate). Today, the number of school leaders who themselves studied Latin – or who understand its educational, linguistic and cognitive value – is in steep decline. It is increasingly difficult to mount a national defence of Latin when few in leadership positions can articulate what would be lost if it disappeared.

My own introduction to Latin was from my prep school headmaster Mr Carnes. Our textbook, Paterson and Macnaughton's *The Approach to Latin* (published in 1938), included sentences that seemed utterly bizarre to a seven-year-old boy. Who on earth says, 'Whither is he hastening?' or 'Why were the sailors laying waste the fields?'.

The textbook's introduction, however, is strikingly clear. It contains this superb explanation for studying Latin:

> Success in Latin is well worth while [sic]. It means that you possess and can use powers of memory, observation and reasoning; it means that you become familiar with the language, literature and history – in fact with the very mind – of one of the most wonderful nations that ever lived; it means you acquire a deeper and wider understanding of English literature and of the English language; it means that you secure a great aid to the learning and real understanding of many modern languages; it means that you can tackle any hard, worth-while job honestly and well.

The authors flag at the outset that mastering Latin is hard. By contrast, modern teaching methods often assume that young people must be entertained; that subjects must be made 'fun' or they will fail. But there is a counterargument, and one that resonates with my experience, that children respond to challenge, to being taken seriously, to being stretched.

Consider the grammatical sophistication required to translate this (from Kennedy's *Shorter Latin Primer*, 1962):

> Labienus, having exhorted the soldiers to keep in mind their former valour and their many successful battles, and to imagine that Caesar, under whose leadership they had to often overcome their foes, was himself present, gives the signal for battle.

I'd wager that few teachers today, let alone students, could correctly identify the grammatical structures and parts of speech in that sentence.

CLASS

We can't ignore the fact that, for centuries, Latin was the gatekeeper to the corridors of power, the libraries of civilisation and intellectual culture generally. Members of the British ruling class – educated at Eton, Harrow, Winchester – were not simply taught to translate Latin; they were taught to *think* in Latin. Older readers will recall the Peter Cook sketch, 'Yes, I could have been a judge, but I never had the Latin.' For those who were classically educated were seen to have a distinct edge. Quite simply, their Latinate syntax, vocabulary and classical allusions set them apart.

And yet, the grammar-school movement of the mid-twentieth century proved that Latin could be democratised. Working-class pupils mastered the third declension and the ablative absolute, and read Virgil. In so doing, they became powerful communicators in English (examples include Bernard Levin, Harold Wilson, Melvyn Bragg and Margaret Thatcher). Today, with Latin vanishing from state schools, we risk recreating this divide. Independent-school students continue getting these benefits while others miss out – feeding again into bigger questions about what kind of society we're building.

THE BENEFITS

So why does Latin matter, then and now? The answer is cognitive, linguistic and pedagogical. Latin teaches precision; it trains students to notice, hear and understand. For example: the difference between who and whom; the semantic difference in English between refuting and rejecting; why enormity is not the same as immensity; and why words like aggravate and decimate are mostly lazily employed. In short, Latin helps us understand the drift of meaning, the structure of grammar and the elegance of linguistic economy. With so much happening in a sentence, it arguably makes us better listeners.

Latin is, in short, a training in *thinking*. And the Renaissance knew this. The *studia humanitatis* – grammar, rhetoric, poetry, history and moral philosophy – were based on Latin. The humanities were designed to form not just scholars but *citizens* – people who could speak, argue, persuade and judge.

Would you rather be operated on by a surgeon who once mastered the intricacies of the Latin third and fourth declensions, or one who never encountered a complex grammatical structure? It's a rhetorical question, but not a trivial one. The habits of mind forged in Latin – care, attention, discipline, synthesis – are transferable.

As the privately educated Dorothy L. Sayers (1947) put it, 'The best grounding for education is the Latin grammar. I say this, not because Latin is traditional and medieval, but simply because even a rudimentary knowledge of Latin cuts down the labour and pains of learning any other subject by at least fifty per cent.'

Even if we accept this as true, the battle for Latin's place in the national curriculum is already lost. The real question now is whether a viable strategy can be developed to preserve Latin as a distinctive component of independent education. Or should the subject be allowed to fade away, as some contend, on the grounds that it reinforces social inequalities and occupies time that could be used more productively?

ETYMOLOGY AND MEANING IN ENGLISH

At the very least, there could be a sector-wide targeted effort to inject a knowledge of core Latin vocabulary into every English curriculum, with a view to unlocking the language's beauty. It is, after all, a part of our 'heritage' (from the Latin *heri* – yesterday). Imaginatively taught, no pupil could fail to be entranced. And let's not forget 'vagina'. It was my prep school science teacher who taught us that *vagina* was Latin for 'sheath' and where one put one's sword.

Similarly, I'd argue that, as a minimum, every student in the country should know, say, 50 or so Greek words in order to unlock everyday words like photography ('writing with light'), democracy ('rule by the people'), metaphor ('to carry beyond'), and so on.

THE FUTURE

The future of Latin hangs in the balance. Independent schools must engage now in a thoughtful and proactive dialogue about whether its place in an ever-crowded curriculum can be justified. Can we articulate a compelling vision for a classical education in the twenty-first century, or is that in fact a contradiction of terms?

One point, based on experience, is that teaching Latin at prep-school level works best with a core cohort that begins around Year 5 and continues, ideally, through Year 8. However, this approach has become challenging as many prep schools now only go to Year 6. For pupils joining a new school in Year 7, the Latin curriculum often restarts from the beginning to accommodate newcomers. Pupil movement during these years has become more fluid, creating real challenges for schools offering the subject, which can only be mastered through methodical progression through sequential stages; skipping content or jumping between levels with gaps in knowledge simply doesn't work.

Excitingly, Latin could thrive in the future through AI instruction and be taught by an enhanced version of Duolingo – and perhaps even more rapidly than other languages since spoken fluency isn't required. An adaptive AI program could preserve Latin the language while a teacher delivered lessons on classical literature and classical civilisation. Latin could be a perfect subject for hybrid learning, with the course easily customised to meet individual learning needs and preferences.

A COURAGEOUS SCHOOL

Consider the story of Catherine Perkins. At her school, St John's in Leatherhead, she was one of only two students taking Latin A-level, and the only student studying Classical Greek. Her school could easily have told her that it was financially unviable to offer these courses. But it didn't; the head took the decision to invest in her. Perkins went on to study classics and now teaches it; she is part of the next generation committed to keeping the classics alive in the independent sector. 'Only now,' she wrote on LinkedIn, 'do I appreciate what it took for those staff individually and for the school as a whole. People fought for my chance. I hope they know it was worth it.'

That was true leadership – and the impact of that school's decision will doubtless be felt for generations to come.

This chapter is more than just a debate about a subject; it touches on our shared values and our vision for education, reimagined for a very different age.

As the Roman poet Horace reminds us, *tempora mutantur, et nos mutamur in illis*: 'Times change, and we change with them'.

ASIDE
WHAT PLAY AM I?

1. I am a British play first performed in 1948, written by a playwright known for his sharp, understated dramas.
2. I am set in an English public school and focus on the life of a retiring classics teacher, a strict and emotionally distant man.
3. A rare moment of kindness comes when one of his pupils gives him a translation of a classical text, moving him deeply.
4. My title refers to an English translation of The Agamemnon by Aeschylus.
5. I was written by the author of *The Winslow Boy* which also has an important role for a schoolboy.

MAGPIE

The magpie is one of the most intelligent and inquisitive birds out there; always poking around new things, sizing up its surroundings with a sharp, thoughtful eye. That same mix of curiosity and clear-headed strategy is what marks out exceptional leadership in independent schools.

All great schools – and all inspiring teachers – share a restless energy. They are always looking to grow, to get better, to see things from fresh angles and, above all, to make every day feel alive and engaging for their students. Just as a parish priest is always keeping an ear out for a good story to slip into Sunday's sermon, a great teacher is a natural collector – of stories, analogies, quirky facts, anything that might spark curiosity.

Teaching, after all, can involve the equivalent of 25 sermons a week. So, the best teachers are always on the hunt for material: a striking line of poetry, a clever metaphor, a linguistic twist, a curious historical detail. These are the raw materials of lively, off-the-cuff teaching. And when the moment's right, the magpie teacher plucks just the right one from memory and brings it to life.

Should the guest speaker at lunch fail to arrive, magpie teachers don't panic. They may even chuckle at the new opportunity which arises. Reaching into their store of ideas, they conjure up an impromptu talk that delights and educates in equal measure. Indeed, this is the very essence of magpie thinking: the readiness to seize an offbeat idea and convert it into something educationally meaningful. If you've ever had the experience of an unexpected 'cover' lesson being one of your best, you'll know what I mean.

Great school leaders are, likewise, collectors. When visiting another school, they scan the walls of the reception area, take in the display boards, notice a novel system or quirky tradition – and make a mental note. They see ideas not as fixed to one context but as ripe for adaptation. Magpie leaders find inspiration in books, conferences, chance conversations and online discussions. But they do not imitate blindly. They discern, evaluate and transpose ideas with judgement and flair. The best leaders, like the most intelligent birds, know what to borrow and what to leave behind.

A GERMAN IDEA TAKES FLIGHT

Sometimes, a single idea, lifted and transplanted, takes root and becomes part of the school's culture. Twenty years ago, while chatting with our German teacher on a summer afternoon, I heard about *Hitzefrei*; a delightful German custom of calling off school during extreme heat. And so, on a sweltering English summer day with laughter on the playing fields and a mood of midsummer magic in the air, I called a *Hitzefrei* and announced that the first lesson after lunch would be cancelled – everyone was to have an extended lunch break.

It was, of course, shamelessly popular and, over the next ten years, our school called a handful of *Hitzefreis*. It became a school tradition and, most important of all, a treasured childhood memory: a moment when the rules bent in favour of joy.

To this day, I wonder what the Department for Education (DfE) would say about it. But this is freedom the independent sector enjoys. Again and again, I find myself looking for 'magic'. Where we can, let's make it. I contend that it is also an intellectual freedom – to buck trends and try new things. We in the independent sector refuse to be constrained by bureaucratic uniformity. Of course we must have timetables, of course we need schemes of work, of course we need structure – but the paradox is that these things are enhanced, not undermined, by occasional spontaneity. The independent school, at its best, is not merely an 'institution' but a living thing: playful, curious, alert, just like the magpie.

THE ECLECTIC SCHOOL

The magpie metaphor serves not only as an image of leadership but also as an ideal for the entire school. The best schools are polymathic, eclectic and intellectually ambitious. They borrow freely: Montessori practices in the early years, Singaporean maths there in KS1, and how about a dash of Steiner or Reggio Emilia over there. There is no single orthodoxy. Instead, there is intelligent synthesis, a tailored curriculum formed by the alchemy of multiple traditions.

Children are, after all, natural magpies: they collect experiences, words, images, questions and facts with insatiable curiosity. The best schools (including, perhaps especially, the most sensitive early years settings) work tirelessly to protect this inborn urge to know, to gather, to dawdle in the garden of knowledge. They delight in the tangential and the arcane. We have all encountered young people where – tragically (and I use the word advisedly) – the joy in learning and discovery has been hollowed out of them. That is not natural; it is their environment that did this.

A magpie curriculum is full of shiny trinkets: obscure historical episodes, curious mathematical paradoxes, fragments of ancient poetry, intriguing philosophical questions. One week, pupils may be exploring Plato's allegory of the cave; the next, they are experimenting with slam poetry, tracing the path of the Voyager probes, learning the Japanese concept of *wabi-sabi* or examining the psychology behind the marshmallow test. They are all part of a broader vision: one in which education is not merely preparation for life, but life itself.

To be a magpie is not to be superficial. On the contrary, it is to possess a cultivated eye for value. In a time of relentless emphasis on measurable outcomes, the magpie reminds us of the joy of the unmeasured thing.

Yet, a word of caution. Not every shiny object is treasure. There is a risk of equating novelty with substance. One can fill a timetable with enrichment activities, clubs and workshops, and yet fail to educate. The wise magpie is selective. Leadership here, as so often the case, is paradoxical – alive to new and spontaneous ideas but also knowing when sustained focus and academic discipline matter most.

THE CONNECTIVE VISION

True magpie schools are not disorderly. They are synthesising forces. In great schools, departments talk to each other and are curious about the work taking place across the school, not just within their own discipline. There is a conscious aim to connect the ideas that have shaped our world.

And so, when Mendeleyev was assembling the periodic table, we know Darwin was setting the world alight over evolution. While Wagner was composing *The Ring*, the Impressionists were reimagining art. While Marx was reshaping political theory, the railways and the Suez Canal were transforming global trade. The magpie school looks at all this and sees not chaos but coherence.

This isn't an 'add-on' activity. It transcends GCSEs, A-levels or any other measurable outcomes. The independent sector's strength is its confidence to fill this cultural and intellectual vacuum and to redefine what an educated mind could be. When this vision is placed at the centre of a school's mission, students learn to connect ideas across disciplines, ask fundamental questions and develop a holistic worldview. This approach to teaching and learning must underpin everything or else the school curriculum is no more than a series of exam syllabuses.

Some will say that times have changed and, in any case, we can look up anything in seconds. Yet we cannot make sense of information unless we understand how it fits into the broader context. It's like being a technically proficient pianist with no understanding of when or where the music you're playing was composed.

BOLD VISION IN A DISTRACTED WORLD

Let's nurture young minds that, like magpies, gather knowledge with joyful, insatiable curiosity; young people who take real pleasure in making sense of the world around them. We want them to explore our cultural and intellectual inheritance, of course, but also to look ahead with excitement and a deep sense of ethical responsibility. Above all, they need to believe – really believe – that they have agency and can shape the future. And with the right encouragement, they will.

There's arguably an existential fight for young souls at present – as anxiety or apathy threaten to take hold. But there's still youthful idealism out there, and it's one of the few forces strong enough to take on the challenges we all face – of widening inequality and growing social division. This is, after all, why we became teachers: not just to impart knowledge, but to shape character and to give young people the confidence to make a difference.

Just as the magpie's bold black-and-white feathers are unmistakable against any backdrop, so too must our educational vision remain compelling – especially today where so much competes for young people's attention. We need to remind ourselves – and remind our students – that real learning isn't about grades, but about turning understanding into purpose and into something that changes the world for the better.

> # ASIDE
> ## WHO AM I?
> 1. I was born in the seventeenth century and became one of the most influential philosophers of the Enlightenment.
> 2. My ideas on education were outlined in a famous work, in which I argued that children are not born with innate knowledge, but rather as a *tabula rasa* (or blank slate).
> 3. I believed that education should focus on developing both the mind and character, rather than just teaching facts and information.
> 4. My views on education influenced later thinkers, such as Jean-Jacques Rousseau, and shaped modern approaches to child development.
> 5. A famous portrait of me, by Godfrey Kneller, hangs in the Hermitage Museum in Saint Petersburg.

NETWORKING

It's not who you know – it's who knows you.

If influence matters (and in today's world, it certainly does), then being 'known' is an asset that can benefit the school community you serve.

But networking isn't just about visibility ('who knows you'), nor is it a vain performance for professional kudos ('look at me, aren't I great?'). Done well, it's about community, authenticity and service. Done poorly, it can make you and your school seem hollow and self-serving. So how should we approach it?

You will have numerous opportunities for professional networking through various school associations, such as HMC (The Heads' Conference), GSA (the Girls' School Association), IAPS (the Independent Association of Prep Schools) and ISA (the Independent Schools Association). These events are generally a joy to attend, not only for the excellent CPD and training courses on offer, but also as a means of meeting and forming professional friendships with heads and senior leaders from different parts of the country.

Always consider, though, whether it's you who really needs to attend a school networking event. If may well be that other members of staff could profitably attend instead. And part of your job is to see them grow in stature and confidence on the schools' circuit.

RAISING YOUR SCHOOL'S PROFILE

These days, if you're the head, you are your school's de facto brand ambassador. Prospective families, future staff, other schools and journalists all take notice of who you are and what you say. The most effective school leaders make networking seem artless, yet beneath the surface, it's deeply strategic.

Keep an eye out for those school leaders who appear regularly in education magazines, write letters to *The Times* or contribute thoughtfully to online debates. These figures raise their schools' profiles, not through self-congratulation but by participating in wider conversations about education. They get noticed because they contribute.

CLUMSY NETWORKING

When networking becomes self-promotion, people notice and it damages your profile. Some leaders get it spectacularly wrong. For heaven's sake, don't describe yourself as 'dynamic', 'inspirational' or 'charismatic'! This is for others to say about you, not for you to say about yourself.

The head who floods social media with photos of themselves standing next to celebrities, who posts every school triumph ('we beat such-and-such school 2–0 in a hard-fought game') as a personal victory, who name-drops constantly or courts journalists with an obvious agenda, is not admired but avoided.

This is where networking turns into vanity. The risk is not only reputational; it's ethical. Leadership – especially school leadership – is about service. If your connections serve only you, and not your school, they become suspect.

And here, it's about looking in the mirror and having an honest conversation with yourself. Is this about you, or is this about your school and community?

AUTHENTICITY MATTERS

Every leader has a different disposition. Some are natural extroverts, energised by events and gatherings. Others are reflective introverts who prefer one-to-one conversations. Most are ambiverts, negotiating the space in between.

Whatever your style, what matters is authenticity. You don't have to network like everyone else. Some of the most effective leaders build smaller, deeper networks. They meet for quiet coffees, invite colleagues for school visits, exchange thoughtful messages and build long-term professional friendships.

Even if you prefer to keep a lower public profile, I recommend being 'quietly active' online, following the latest education stories as they break and keeping abreast of current educational data. In just five minutes a day, with judicious scrolling, you can cover a huge amount of ground, pick up numerous new ideas, articles to read, book recommendations, and often get an international perspective on the education topic of the day, whether that's AI assessment or recruitment strategies for physics teachers.

Follow the national debates, know the thought leaders and understand the evolving educational discourse. You can lurk rather than post, but by opting out completely, you're going to lose far more than you gain.

YOUR SCHOOL COMES FIRST – IN EVERYTHING

Some leaders get this balance wrong. Somehow they're off at dinners and conferences, or away on trips, supposedly doing important things but unseen in their own corridors. Staff comment that the head is always elsewhere, attending yet another leadership symposium or podcast interview – and the school feels it.

The internal network matters more. Relationships with staff, students and parents are not just important – they are the core of the job. A great deal of your best networking will be done in the lunch queue, waiting in line with students, at the school gate or walking with a colleague to the car park at the end of the day.

So, is spending hours at yet another networking event *really* the best use of your precious, precious time? Think carefully whether you can justify the time away, especially if it involves significant travel time. School leadership is local. If you want to be known nationally, be certain you are known first and foremost by your own community.

To be blunt – the head who is too busy broadcasting their leadership may not be doing enough of it.

KNOW YOUR STRATEGY

The worst strategy is no strategy. Some heads bumble through their professional networks with vague intentions. It is far better to be deliberate.

Start by mapping your local schools (use *The Good Schools Guide* 'find a school' option to see all the schools within a 1-, 3- and 5-mile radius). Over time, reach out and visit them all. Ask your PA to schedule short tours or lunch meetings. Getting to know your local heads is a game-changer – and the more supportive you are of each other, the better. In wanting the best for your students and for your community, your authenticity will shine through on the circuit. At one level you may be competitors in a market, but forming professional friendships with other heads means they're more likely to become potential allies. Remember, too, that a handwritten card still packs a punch if you want to send a note of thanks!

Know your local paper. Some heads even contribute regular columns to their local newspaper, offering educational insights or community commentary. Your school should have a quiet but consistent presence in the local media.

Develop relationships with local journalists and know who all the education journalists are in the mainstream media (ITV, BBC, Sky, all the broadsheets). By connecting online, via X or LinkedIn, you'll always be up to speed with current educational developments and, over time, you'll notice those journalists with whom you have an affinity. If you admire someone's work, tell them.

As far as is reasonable or practical, it's worth getting to know the businesses in your area – especially the smaller or family-owned ones. And don't forget estate agents, who are often first-contact points for relocating families. A good relationship can bring prospective parents to your door. Local gyms, cafés and dry cleaners might offer staff discounts, strengthening your school's role in the community. None of these things may be a priority as such but, over time, they add up and strengthen your school's position within the community.

Beware the tendency to associate only with those like yourself – potentially a danger in the independent sector. It narrows horizons and fosters a certain conformity. Actively seek out dialogue with those in state schools, international schools and even other industries. As ever, keep an ear and eye out for potential partnerships and synergies.

LinkedIn remains powerful for educational networking. Used well, it helps you follow research, connect with leaders across sectors and stay visible. LinkedIn has also proven to be a fast and cost-effective way of sourcing teachers during staffing crises. X, once dominant, has waned for some, but other forums exist. Beware of the echo chamber. Online spaces can quickly become performative. Share because it helps others, not to chase likes. And – of course – always ask permission before posting photos with colleagues (or anyone else for that matter).

Every conversation you have is a chance to tell your school's story. Not a marketing pitch, but a reflection of your values and purpose. The best networkers are also great storytellers: they are vivid, honest and memorable. Including a snippet of local history or a relevant literary anecdote can elevate your message above the banal.

Networking matters. But it is not leadership. Leadership is not abstract. It is shaped in quiet decisions, not loud events.

In the end, your best networking is done in the ordinary encounters of school life: the corridor conversation, the thank-you note, the mentoring moment. Get that right, and everything else becomes easier.

SUMMARY

- **Be intentional.** Develop a networking strategy. Put it in writing and revisit it regularly.
- **Raise your school's profile.** But make sure your motives are right.
- **Stay rooted.** Internal connections matter most.
- **Be authentic.** Align your networking style with your character.
- **Visit nearby schools.** Get to know the local heads.
- **Connect locally.** Know your neighbours, local businesses and journalists.
- **Diversify.** Seek out connections in the state sector. Look for possible synergies.
- **Tell your school's story.** Let your values shine through.

In short, networking is not about being everywhere. It's about being known, trusted and useful in the right places. Done well, it can amplify your leadership and enrich your school. But never forget: the best connections start close to home.

ASIDE

WHO AM I?

1. I founded a progressive school for peasant children on my family estate in the 1860s, focusing on freedom in learning.
2. I wrote extensively on education, arguing that teachers should respect children's individuality and curiosity, rather than impose rigid structures.
3. My school had no punishments, no rigid schedules and no forced memorisation, making it highly radical for its time.
4. I published *The ABC Book* (*Azbuka*) and other materials aimed at making literacy accessible to Russia's peasants.
5. I also wrote novels. One of them led to my being excommunicated by the Russian Orthodox Church.

OOMPH

School leadership demands an extraordinary reservoir of energy. The job can't be done unless there exists deep within you a fundamental drive and instinct to push forwards. There are doubtless echoes of Freudian theory here where libido is sublimated into leadership energy. But this 'oomph' isn't merely theoretical: workforce statistics show that headteachers take fewer sick days than classroom teachers or middle leaders. One eminent head with a famously booming voice told me he'd only taken one day off in 35 years!

This dedication carries risks, though. Presenteeism can prove dangerous when it means working through illness or ignoring symptoms. And while heads may be absent less frequently, they face greater risk of burnout and stress-induced early retirement. Nevertheless, let's establish that oomph is vital – and more is better than less.

The head's oomph is often decisive for parents choosing a school. Whether in one-on-one conversations or addressing large audiences, a leader's authentic energy is unmistakable. This isn't about charisma; it's about the drive to make difficult decisions, the spark to inspire others and the persistence to maintain standards of excellence.

The number one task for any head is to appoint, develop and retain a stellar teaching team, much as a Premier League manager must grow and develop elite players. The parallel is apt: teachers' success in the classroom reflects directly on the head's leadership, as does failure. When teachers deliver lessons with élan, the head's vision takes tangible form; but if teachers are cynical and disaffected, questions inevitably arise about leadership.

Just walk past any classroom door during lessons and watch. (The finest teachers often teach with their doors open as if to say 'come in and join us'.) Within seconds, student body language tells you everything. Are students leaning forward and engaged? Or are they slumped in boredom? Teens don't hide what they think.

Leadership means making tough calls that nobody else wants to make. Underperforming teachers deserve compassionate support and a chance to improve. But if that improvement doesn't materialise, they need to go (though always gently and with care). This is where oomph becomes essential – having the nous to address difficult issues directly rather than sweeping them under the carpet or just hoping they'll somehow resolve themselves.

Effective leadership means having the oomph and the wisdom to know when and how to ask those questions that make people uncomfortable. If this is not your forte, then daily life provides opportunities to practise: politely questioning an incorrect restaurant bill, disputing a parking ticket or asking a lout to take their feet off a train seat. Each instance serves as an opportunity to develop your oomph; to develop the presence and skills you can use in your work life.

Successful heads embody two seemingly contradictory traits: a gentle, approachable manner balanced with inner steel and unstoppable drive. This combination creates an unmistakable determination that people can sense immediately, even from a distance. Their warmth invites connection, while their resolve inspires confidence and commitment.

AUDITING YOUR OOMPH

How much oomph do you (and your senior colleagues) possess? Score yourself honestly on a scale of 1 (low) to 10 (high), then ask yourself:

- What score would your colleagues give you? What about your students and your parents?
- Are you satisfied with their perception of your energy, presence and impact?

Developing oomph means amplifying your authentic self to become the best version of you on whatever stage you occupy: your classroom, your school or the wider community.

CORE COMPONENTS OF OOMPH

Presence: do you own the room?
- When you enter a space, do people instinctively look up, or do you fade into the background?
- Do you exude energy and confidence, even under pressure?
- If you were a student or teacher, would you want to follow yourself?

Delivery: can you command attention?
- Do you speak with conviction, or do you sometimes sound hesitant or monotonous?
- Do people lean in when you speak or are they tuning out?
- If you were giving a speech and the microphone failed, could you hold the room with just your voice and presence?

Style: does your appearance reflect your leadership?
- Do your clothes communicate 'purposeful leader'?
- Do you dress intentionally to reinforce your message and personality?
- Would a first impression based solely on appearance suggest 'here's a person with oomph'?

Energy: are you electrifying?
- How often do you energise a room rather than drain it?
- Would your team describe you as a motivator or merely a manager?
- Do you arrive at school each day with robust optimism?
- How frequently do you take calculated risks to inject creativity and joy into your school's culture?

Authenticity: do you come across as real or rehearsed?
- Do you lead from your true self or are you performing a role? Can you distinguish between the two?

- In your connections with others, are you genuine or do you rely on safe, scripted interactions?
- Would colleagues and students describe you as 'real' or 'guarded'?

Influence: do you leave a mark?
- What do you do daily that people will remember next week – or next year?
- When you speak or act, do you inspire or confuse?
- Are you a leader who moves mountains – or one who just sends emails?

Feedback: do you seek it or avoid it?
- When did you last request brutally honest feedback? Did you act on it or dismiss it?
- Do you know what your team says about you when you're not present? Would their words inspire or mortify you?
- Have you created a culture where people feel safe to tell you when you've lost your spark? What about when you've made a mistake?

The X-factor: what sets you apart?
- What one thing distinguishes you from every other leader?
- How often do you positively surprise people?
- Do you embrace your unique strengths and quirks, or try to conform to generic leadership stereotypes?

Legacy: what do you want people to say about you?
- If you left your role tomorrow, what would staff and students miss most about you?
- Are you building a leadership legacy, or just getting through each day?
- What has been your most impactful 'oomph moment' so far, and when will the next one occur?

Resolute self-care: do you have the oomph to manage yourself?
- Are you modelling self-discipline in diet, sleep and fitness?

- Do you treat your mental and physical health as non-negotiable, or sacrifice it for work?
- How can you expect to inspire discipline in others if you neglect your own wellbeing?

CHALLENGE YOURSELF TO GROW

None of us can stay on top of everything at all times. So it's as well to take stock from time to time.

1. **Identify your gaps**: which questions above made you uncomfortable? That discomfort indicates where your greatest growth potential lies.
2. **Take bold action**: commit to one courageous step this week to elevate your oomph.

Whatever your starting point, oomph can be developed. More importantly, it *must* be developed. There can be no excuse for just jogging along without improvements.

OOMPH IN PRACTICE

A teacher once shared with me her dread of parents' evenings. She particularly dreaded facing certain challenging parents who left her feeling bruised. She decided to reframe these encounters as exciting growth opportunities – chances to develop skills that would benefit her entire life. Rather than fearing difficult parents, she began to see them as her greatest teachers. Over time, this intentional mindset shift transformed her approach and dramatically increased her confidence and effectiveness.

When reviewing recordings of my first radio interviews, I was dismayed by my verbal tics and filler words. Through ruthless self-assessment and practice, I've improved significantly. Even today, I discreetly record every speech to identify further refinements. A continuous self-improvement cycle can apply to every aspect of our professional lives – if we genuinely want to improve.

Oomph never means seeking the spotlight; it's about generating purposeful energy that transcends yourself. It's the quiet confidence that allows you to step back and let others shine, knowing your influence doesn't diminish when shared – it multiplies. Your oomph creates a ripple effect, inspiring others to discover their own version.

ASIDE

WHO AM I?

1. I was born in 1886 in Germany and had a privileged upbringing, receiving an elite education in Germany and the UK.
2. I founded a progressive school in Germany in the 1920s, emphasising leadership, responsibility and outdoor education.
3. The rise of the Nazi regime forced me into exile, where I established a similar school in Scotland – Gordonstoun.
4. My educational philosophy inspired the creation of institutions like Outward Bound, the United World Colleges and the Duke of Edinburgh's Award.
5. I believed in a set of principles designed to counteract the decline of modern youth, including moral courage, self-discipline and compassion.

PARENTS

It helps to really like parents – all parents! Never forget, even for a moment, the trust they place in you. They've handed over the most precious part of their lives and are paying a considerable sum of money for the privilege. That alone demands respect – deep, sincere and ongoing respect. In any case, respect is essential – for communication, for partnership, for trust.

RESPECT, RESPECT, RESPECT

Parents in independent schools are typically highly intelligent, articulate and accomplished. They expect a first-class education for their child. They can't be fobbed off; they know what 'good' looks like. It is essential, therefore, to understand the underlying dynamics of the parent–school relationship.

While teachers and middle leaders may not ponder too much the financial commitment of parents, a good head always does. Something not often understood by those outside the independent sector is quite how daunting these fees are for many parents. In my 20 years of independent school leadership, I have had dealings with hundreds of families quietly struggling to pay.

Today, it is not uncommon for grandparents or other family members to help, where they can, with fees. Of course, some parents are wealthy but many make sacrifices – like the mother who chose not to travel to India for her own mother's funeral, so carefully was she conserving funds for the next term's fees. That moment has stayed with me.

Modern life being what it is, many parents are stressed and time-poor – and feel guilty about not spending enough time with their children. Understanding this context makes it easier to decode certain behaviours. The angry email about a last-minute change to a netball fixture might seem disproportionate – until you remember the logistical juggle, the emotional load and the financial commitment that underpins everything.

Good leadership doesn't dismiss these moments. It engages with them thoughtfully.

> **TIP**
>
> If a family is in financial difficulty, that's not the business of teaching staff. But it should be shared on a need-to-know basis with members of the senior leadership team, such as the head of pastoral care, as financial strains at home can affect a pupil's wellbeing.

NOT JUST CLIENTS

Yes, parents are clients – but they're also partners, critics, supporters and ambassadors.

As head, you're not merely responding to issues – you're building long-term relationships. This is why working through challenges should be viewed as an opportunity to deepen connections – especially when guiding parties toward mutual understanding.

Meanwhile, a reassuring word at drop-off, a quick phone call or a kind aside after assembly can do more for the school's reputation than any marketing material.

> **TIP**
>
> When scheduled to meet a 'difficult' or dissatisfied parent, avoid dreading the encounter or labelling them in your mind as 'a nightmare parent'. Such thinking sets you up for failure. Your body language will almost certainly betray your thoughts, undermining any chance of connection or resolution.

FORM TUTORS

Especially in a prep school, your form tutors shape parents' views about the school culture. They're front-line listeners, pastoral leaders and are often instrumental in whether or not a pupil likes school. They need judgement about when to escalate concerns, when to reassure and how to read a parent's mood. Don't assume that tutors will just learn on the job, or 'get better' on their own. Gather them regularly, share expertise and experiences, and actively support those with development needs.

Your parents will sense whether or not their pupil's tutor is engaging at a heartfelt level – or whether they are just following school policy.

PARENTS LEARN TOO

In all-through schools, you'll notice that the parental relationship evolves as pupils mature. Parents of younger pupils tend to be anxious and deeply involved. As pupils progress, parents gradually step back. But if you've done things right by then, trust is established. That quiet confidence is your reward.

Beware the so-called 80/20 rule, or Pareto principle, where 20% of your parents account for 80% of all incoming concerns, complaints and special requests! And while you might quite rightly spend more time engaging with some parents, don't neglect the 'middle 80%' – those whose children neither struggle academically nor are winning scholarships. In fact, go further than this – value this middle 80% consciously. They are the backbone of your school. Never take them for granted

PROACTIVE ENGAGEMENT

Don't wait for problems. Glance down the school list. When did you last speak to that parent? If it has been five terms, make contact. A quick invitation to discuss their child's experience – particularly when things are going well – can really boost the relationship with the parents.

What looks like parental aloofness can mask uncertainty, or even fear. One father, who rarely visited the school, told me that he'd had such a traumatic experience of school himself that just stepping foot in one today made him physically sick. Reaching out changed everything.

Online safety evenings, parent evenings and similar events create moments of cohesion. That said, be realistic. The parents who most need your wisdom are usually the ones who don't turn up. Ask yourself, how will you reach them?

DIFFICULT CONVERSATIONS

There is a peculiar satisfaction in mastering difficult conversations. I may be a masochist, but I came to value them. They sharpen your skills, protect your staff and preserve the school's integrity.

Be guided by principles not by emotion. When a father was rude to our lovely receptionist, I made sure to meet him myself. Calmly, without anger or accusation, I listened. I wanted to understand. His behaviour was totally unacceptable, but my approach led him to reflect, apologise and bring flowers. I didn't demand it. I didn't need to.

> **TIP**
>
> Since about 2015, I always assumed meetings might be recorded. I never knew if they were, but the thought sharpened my thinking.

Golden rules:

- Never speak negatively of one family to another.
- Don't be drawn into gossip or triangulation.
- Stick to facts. Speak calmly. Let parents finish. Take notes.

COMPLAINTS

When complaints come – as they will – listen carefully. Write things down. The act of putting pen to paper demonstrates to parents that you're taking them seriously; it almost always calms things down and prepares the ground for resolution. At the end of the meeting, read your notes back to confirm accuracy.

Then breathe. Escalation helps no one. Sometimes a heartfelt apology, even when technically unnecessary, defuses the situation with dignity.

Your body language matters. Your tone matters. Your choice of words matters. And silence, when used well, is powerful. Ask open, non-defensive questions:

- What is your understanding of what happened?
- What is important to you here?

You're not aiming to win the argument. You're aiming to understand – and resolve. In emotionally charged situations, leave Cartesian logic at the door. No parent wants to be proved wrong. Remember the adage that, 'People will forget what you said, people will forget what you did, but people will never forget how you made them *feel*.'

Better to say, 'Given what you knew at the time, I can see why you felt that way. But now, looking at the full picture …'

Watch their body language; it reveals whether they're relaxing, opening up or preparing to push back.

LANGUAGE

Language shapes outcomes. Don't have 'difficult' conversations; have important ones. Never tell a parent, 'You don't understand'; say 'I haven't explained myself clearly enough.'

Remember that there are no 'problems', only challenges. It's important to cascade this kind of nuance – this detailed attention to language – throughout your organisation.

Communication is a skill that can be learned and refined. Whatever your current ability, you can be better next year. That's part of your professional development.

MEETINGS

Not everything requires a meeting. Sometimes a call or email is best. When you do meet:

- Avoid sitting behind a desk – it creates a barrier.
- Watch out for low chairs that diminish the parent's presence.
- Let your office speak of reflection: books, journals, thoughtfulness. A head without bookshelves is merely renting the title.

WHEN IT BREAKS DOWN

Occasionally, and very sadly, the relationship with a family breaks down beyond repair. In such cases, remain calm and firm. Seek legal advice. Document everything. Offer dignified exits – and protect your community. Offer support to any staff member who may have been affected by the fallout.

Never send an email in anger. Review your first draft and remove any emotive language. Always write with the assumption that a judge, the media or ISI/Ofsted may later read your words.

Don't beat yourself up. Sometimes you may have made a mistake, from which you can learn, but other times these things can't be avoided. Absorbing, and learning from these moments, is part of headship.

SPECIAL CASES

You may have famous parents. Treat them like everyone else; or better, treat everyone like them. Never mention them outside school.

With international parents, be clear about notice periods and financial commitments. Misunderstandings over the term's notice in lieu of fees are common. Consider having translations available of key contractual terms.

A few parents will be genuinely difficult. A small minority (just 1–2% in my experience) may display emotional volatility or manipulative behaviour. It's worth reading about Cluster B personality disorders – you'll begin to recognise patterns.

And yet – be kind. These people may be deeply unhappy. Often their child pays the price. Compassion is part of your leadership.

DELEGATION

You cannot handle every case. Identify staff who can. Coach them. Share your experience. Help them learn how to de-escalate and connect.

You are not the only relationship-builder in the school. Build a team that can do this well.

PARENTS GROW TOO

In a great school, students flourish. But so do parents. They grow in trust, understanding and confidence. You may have been through tough times together. That, too, is part of your work.

Listen. Take notes. Honour their investment. And remember – every parental encounter is a chance to model and transmit the culture of your school.

Parents don't buy services. They buy understanding.

ASIDE

WHO AM I?

1. I was a psychologist and educational theorist born in the early twentieth century, whose ideas have had a lasting impact on how children learn.
2. One of my most famous concepts is the 'Zone of Proximal Development' (ZPD), which describes the gap between what a learner can do independently and what they can achieve with guidance.
3. I believed that learning is fundamentally a social process and that children develop higher cognitive functions through interactions with teachers, parents and peers.
4. Unlike theorists who emphasised fixed developmental stages, I argued that learning drives development, rather than the other way around.
5. I introduced the idea of 'scaffolding,' where a knowledgeable guide provides structured support to help a learner progress until they can work independently.

QUIRKINESS

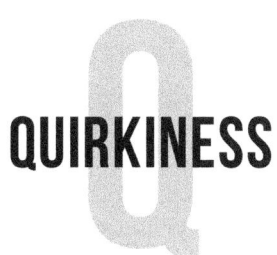

With a fine disregard for the rules ...

In 1823, a boy at Rugby School called William Webb Ellis picked up the football and ran with it. And in that single, rule-breaking moment – equal parts mischief and originality – the game of rugby was born.

The phrase hovers somewhere in the DNA of all great independent schools: a fine disregard for the rules. Not in the anarchic sense – and absolutely not in the regulatory compliance or safeguarding sense – but as a cultural instinct to value imagination over obedience, and individuality over conformity. And if we are serious about producing free-thinking, morally courageous, intellectually lively young people, then we should be equally serious about defending the right of schools – and teachers – to be just a little bit odd.

ECCENTRICITY

English independent schools have always been slightly eccentric. That's part of their charm. Consider Christ's Hospital with its Tudor uniforms and signature yellow stockings, or the many schools that preserve their own esoteric sporting traditions – reminiscent of Quidditch at Hogwarts. How about the 'Greaze' at Westminster School – a Shrove Tuesday tradition in which boys scramble beneath a metal bar to catch pieces of a horsehair-laced pancake tossed by the school cook? But there's method in the madness, for somewhere deep down, we know that these whacky traditions create shared joy, lasting memories and a camaraderie. These are every bit as important as what's on the school curriculum. The educational experience is found in the whole.

The eccentricity isn't just in the rituals, but in the people: the classics teacher who, on the Ides of March, delivers his lesson in spoken Latin; the physics teacher who cycles at speed past his students in his flowing gown, blasting his horn, to illustrate the Doppler effect; the art teacher who brought in a dead dog for the students to sketch. And while such teachers are sometimes maddening for school leadership to manage, they bring much entertainment and joy into the students' lives.

QUIRKINESS AND FREE THINKING

Research in psychology consistently shows links between traits associated with quirkiness and creative or original thinking. While not every eccentric is a genius, there is a notable statistical correlation between high creative output and behavioural divergence from the norm.

We mustn't limit our view of quirkiness to the traditions of England. It takes many forms, and in a truly inclusive educational setting, it flourishes across cultures, backgrounds, languages and neurotypes. The primary school teacher who, instead of keeping it hidden, chooses once in a while to delight her pupils by speaking Jamaican Patois; or the supply teacher from New Zealand who, in her short time at the school, taught her year group how to perform the haka. These are some real-life examples of the same spirit. Quirkiness isn't heritage-specific. It's human – and it must be valued, not hemmed in.

A quick search on Google Scholar throws up numerous studies evidencing the link between quirkiness and memorable teaching. This abstract from a 2024 study by Tidy & Irving-Walton expresses the idea quite brilliantly:

> If you think about your own experiences of learning there are probably moments that stand out, experiences that stay with you and improbable links that helped concepts fall into place. These memorable moments are often surprising, frequently entertaining but always relevant. Behind the scenes creating these hooks is a skill and an art in itself – the ability of a subject specialist to make their subject come to life.
>
> These 'quirky' approaches to learning and teaching don't always fall into a specific area of pedagogical practice – they can be simple or complex, a bit of a twist on a well-known strategy

or a completely new take. They can involve applying common approaches in novel ways or being a magpie and shaping ideas gleaned from elsewhere to your own learning environments.

It's often through these moments that the thinking, the personality and enthusiasm of the [teacher] shines through. Modelling for students not just how to apply knowledge and skills but also how to take pleasure in the process. Quirky approaches can add a degree of levity to the learning environment whilst encouraging students to view the subject at hand from a range of angles. This helps build breadth and understanding, encourages experimentation and independence and creates an enriched student – and staff – experience.

Public figures like physicist Brian Cox, whose rock musician background and wonder-filled explanations of the cosmos transfix us in a state of awe, or Cambridge classicist Mary Beard, who brings the ancient world vividly to life on television, stand as advertisements for intellectual quirkiness. And let's not forget dear Sister Wendy Beckett, a cloistered nun turned art historian and unlikely TV star, who embodied a kind of quiet, radiant eccentricity.

What unites them is not just their flair for performance, but their ability to teach in a way that is emotionally charged, deeply human and often off-beat; the kind of teaching that can electrify a young person's imagination in ways that (we hope) no AI will ever quite replicate.

The bottom line is that schools that embrace at least a degree of quirkiness are more likely to produce innovative outcomes. And this is where the independent sector has traditionally had the edge – not simply because of resources or buildings, but because of the space it affords to personality.

And yet, arguably, that space is under threat. The professionalisation of the teaching profession over the last 25 years has undoubtedly brought necessary improvements – such as the firm policies in place around health and safety, and safeguarding. And today it is a school leader's absolute duty to keep a secure eye on their self-evaluation form (SEF) and prepare comprehensively for inspections. The risk, however, is that in so doing, they inadvertently (or even deliberately) brush away some of the magic.

I've often had fascinating, wide-ranging discussions with young, sparkling newly qualified teachers (NQTs) only to then observe them enter classrooms, dutifully post learning objectives, open a PowerPoint and deliver predictable three-part lessons. What a loss.

It is the teachers with character that students remember most – like the teacher who suddenly stopped mid-sentence at the distant sound of a lawnmower, only to leave the classroom, berate the groundsman for interrupting his flow, and return five minutes later to resume exactly where he left off. These human interactions create drama and amusement in students' lives – and they're precisely what cannot be emulated by AI or standardised teaching methods.

It is what allows a prep school teacher to digress wildly from the curriculum – say, to teach Goethe's *Erlkönig* to Year 4 in German (!) as well as in parallel translation. This is education as adventure, drama and joy. Not every lesson should be like this, of course. But some should. Otherwise, what are we doing?

HOW MUCH ROPE?

Quirky teachers are adored by their students and make school an unforgettable experience. But there is always a line. An effective school leader asks: how much rope do I give this teacher? And the answer is: *just* enough. Enough to allow the personality to breathe, the passion to spark – but not so much that the school loses coherence. For sure, there will be times when you'll need to rein them in. It's a balance. But one worth getting right. Quirkiness, when grounded in knowledge and love of subject, is not a liability. It is a differentiator.

Some schools institutionalise their quirks. Hill House in London – where students wear distinctive knee breeches modelled on the founder's climbing attire, complemented by gold jumpers and cravats – is a visual manifesto of ethos. The founders famously declared, 'A grey uniform produces grey minds'. And while it may look eccentric in 2025, the principle is deadly serious: schools must foster character, not conformity.

Other schools express their quirkiness through curricular risk: those secondary schools with lessons starting later in the morning for teenagers (based, incidentally, on solid neuroscience regarding adolescent circadian rhythms); imaginative use of the Harkness method; chess formally timetabled on the primary years curriculum (an idea borrowed from the Soviet Union); a fully bilingual early years setting. These are not frivolities. They are ways in which a school proclaims, 'We think differently'.

Even quirky externalities – a peculiar colour scheme, a double-decker bus converted to a library, a shell grotto, an outdoor amphitheatre, a resident flock of wild parakeets – can signal to pupils that they are in a place where being something different matters.

THE SMALL-SCHOOL ADVANTAGE

It's worth noting, too, that some of the more characterful schools in the independent sector are small. According to the DfE, around 40% of independent schools have fewer than 100 pupils.

In these smaller schools, personalities can truly shine, and a teacher, even a short-term one, can make a huge impact. These schools may be vulnerable when key staff leave, and they may lack the polish of their larger cousins, but they are also places where quirky traditions take root more easily and become part of the school's identity. Where the school dog sits in on assembly and becomes truly the school mascot – childhood memories that last a lifetime.

A LEADERSHIP CHECKLIST

- **Are you hiring for personality as well as proficiency?** Do your recruitment processes allow room for idiosyncrasy and genuine passion?
- **Have you made space for the eccentric within your school culture?** Are there traditions, rituals or visual cues that tell students that they're in a place that values individuality?
- **Do your teaching standards and professional development encourage risk and spontaneity – or inhibit it?** Are your CPD frameworks wide enough to include experimentation, creativity and joyful digression?

- **Are your teachers bringing themselves into the room?** Are they allowed (and encouraged) to be surprising, vivid and memorable – in ways that deepen learning?
- **Have you institutionalised any of your quirks?** Do you honour the peculiarities of your setting – whether it's a school dog, a pancake toss or a striking sports strip – as emblems of character?
- **Is joy visible in the learning?** Can a visitor see, hear or feel the joy of discovery, playfulness or creative mischief in your classrooms?

The distinctive character of independent education lies not in uniformity but in our courage to be different. It takes a confident school and a confident leader to preserve this spirit, that has shaped generations of free thinkers, innovators and leaders.

And sometimes – just sometimes – that means picking up the ball and running with it.

ASIDE

WHAT NOVEL AM I?

1. I am set in an exclusive private school for girls in Scotland, where discipline, tradition and propriety are highly valued.
2. At this school, students are expected to follow strict academic standards, but my central character defies convention by focusing on art, history and her personal philosophies.
3. Rather than preparing her students solely for exams, my teacher selects a special group of girls – her 'set' – and grooms them to embrace her views on life, culture and even politics.
4. The curriculum in this elite private school is traditional, but my protagonist dismisses rigid learning in favour of storytelling, travels and admiration of great men.
5. A betrayal from within her inner circle leads to her downfall, as the private school's leadership ultimately decides she is too radical to remain in her position.

REFLECTIVENESS

As independent school leaders, our days are jam-packed. There is always more to do than there is time to do it. We're fine at managing all the usual things: chairing meetings, zipping through emails, interviewing new students, reviewing budgets with the bursar, and so on. Ideally, even as head, you maintain teaching commitments – often the highlight of the day!

But the weightier stuff that comes with leadership can be emotionally draining: demanding parents, safeguarding issues, cash-flow concerns, meetings with parents in financial difficulties, addressing potential legal matters. The list is endless. But you can't do any of this effectively, unless you are in the habit of being actively reflective. The key word here, as with so many aspects of leadership, is *habit*.

To lead effectively, you must set aside time – preferably daily – for reflection. This means dedicating 20 minutes to sitting back and processing the events of the past 24 hours while looking ahead at what's coming. This vital practice allows you to check in with yourself, assessing where you stand emotionally, physically and spiritually. Additionally, a once-a-week review helps ensure you maintain perspective on all your personal and professional goals.

This practice isn't about doing anything, or crossing items off your to-do list; it's about accurate self-assessment. Only when you've captured all the distractions, loose thoughts and unresolved issues in your life can you achieve the calm, thoughtfulness and reflective capacity needed to make sound decisions.

Each person's ideal reflection time differs. For me, during the working week, 5.30am is optimal. I make a coffee and sit with pen and notebook to review the previous day's events and briefly preview the day ahead. Then the next 20 minutes is 'my time'. If you're running a complex organisation like a school, I'd argue that this practice isn't optional – it's essential for effective leadership.

For some, this will be a time for prayer. For others, it involves quiet reading. I always keep certain materials at hand: Marcus Aurelius' *Meditations*, a poetry anthology (*Poem for the Day: One*) and a little book called *Meditations for Men Who Do Too Much*. (There's a version for women as well.) Countless similar resources exist to support this practice.

This daily reset is invaluable because, like mindfulness practice, it makes you fully conscious of the present moment and your place within it. Such reflective practice is essential in school leadership because it helps you remain aware of how you're using each moment of your day. It's especially important to consider how much of your time is spent:

- dealing with important day-to-day issues connected with the smooth operation of the school that absolutely require your attention
- reflecting on the school's longer-term needs and what steps you can take (however small) today to move the school closer to its strategic goals.

Occasionally, especially in my early days as a headmaster, a day would unfold dominated by the first category: meeting parents, leading assemblies, teaching classes, resolving staffing issues, and so on. But this isn't headship. Over time, I became more skilled at dedicating my time to activities in the second category: the meetings, decisions and planning that would propel the school forward. Others might not immediately notice significant improvements in the school's standing, reputation or effectiveness on any given day, but I knew we were progressing steadily toward our goals.

If you haven't already, try to develop this kind of awareness about how you spend your time each day. Reflect daily on whether you're achieving the right ratio of activities for what you ultimately need to accomplish. This simple practice may be the most powerful leadership tool you never knew you needed.

SEEING YOURSELF CLEARLY

One of the great paradoxes of leadership is that everyone's watching you – but you're the last to see yourself clearly. We all have blind spots, which is why tools like the Johari Window can be so powerful.

The Johari Window		
	Known to self	**Not known to self**
Known to others	ARENA What you and others know about yourself	BLIND SPOT What others know about you that you don't
Not known to others	FAÇADE What you know about yourself that others don't	UNKNOWN Your unconscious self (not known by you or others)

Sharing the Johari Window with all staff encourages a school-wide awareness that we all have different aspects to ourselves: an 'arena' where our interests and traits are known both to us and others; a 'façade' where we know things about ourselves that others don't; and, importantly, a 'blind spot' where others perceive, see and know things about us that we ourselves cannot see. Over time, use of the Johari Window leads to higher levels of organisational sensitivity, and a greater openness to (gently given) feedback.

But of course, all this must come from the top. If you want a reflective, thoughtful, gently questioning school, then this must be modelled by the school leadership. Over time, you'll be able to open up honest conversations around feedback and self-awareness. But if you don't invite others to reflect with you, you'll miss the whole picture.

It's well worth investing from time to time in 360-degree feedback services too. Painful? Sometimes. But if approached with maturity, it can be transformational.

We are all of us on a journey – towards greater self-awareness and more effective interactions with others. Looking back, I wince at some of my past actions, though these growth stories often inspire others to become more receptive to feedback themselves. One of my worst faux pas was in my twenties as a young teacher directing a George Bernard Shaw play.

Noticing an empty space on the back of the programme, I had what seemed like a bright idea: to add a Shaw quotation, 'He who can, does; he who cannot, teaches.' The play went down a storm. The quotation? Not so much. I had completely overlooked how my (older) colleagues might feel about this particular sentiment – something a more reflective version of me would (I hope) have anticipated.

CULTURE STARTS AT THE TOP

A reflective culture doesn't appear out of nowhere – it's modelled by the head. That means no one gets to walk around thinking, 'I'm right'. Instead, we create environments where staff feel safe to ask questions, offer ideas and admit when something isn't working. This doesn't mean indecision. Rather, it's normalising dialogue as essential practice. Reflection, at its best, becomes a team activity.

I once had a new teacher email a scathing message to a colleague in anger. It had to be addressed. But the real issue wasn't the email, it was the emotional reactivity behind it. In reflective schools, we challenge behaviour like this not with censoriousness or a verbal warning, but with a gentle, connective conversation (and always seeking first to understand). That's the difference between reacting and responding.

EMOTIONAL INTELLIGENCE

Anyone who works in schools deals with the full gamut of human emotion: grief, elation, rage, fear, hope. We see students struggling with mental health, colleagues buckling under personal stress, families in turmoil. And sometimes, we're the ones falling apart.

It's critical to recognise when you're not in a place to make good decisions. My PA once said to me, 'You know you're not the person to deal with this right now'. She was right. I was exhausted, emotionally depleted, and in that state, I was likely to escalate, not resolve the situation. Are you able to have appropriate, trust-filled conversations with colleagues about your emotional threshold? Do you have colleagues who know you well enough to tell you when you're off balance? And can you do the same for them?

WHAT'S REALLY DRIVING YOU?

Leadership in independent schools can be seductive. The prestige, the history, the rituals. But it's worth pausing to ask – why are you doing this?

For some, it's the chance to make a difference. For others, it's about tradition, ambition or even redemption. None of these motives is inherently wrong, but if you're not clear about them, they can lead you astray. Are you running your school to serve or to be seen? Are you genuinely giving others wings, or quietly taking centre stage?

PERSONAL LIFE

Your personal life affects your leadership. Fact. If your marriage is falling apart, if you're not sleeping, if you're drinking too much, if your children barely see you – these things will surface. Maybe not today, but eventually.

One of the most valuable things you can do as a leader is to stay grounded. Protect time with your family. Don't skip medical appointments. Get help if you need it. Avoid drinking at school events; it only takes one too many for people to lose respect. Remember: everyone is watching, all the time. That's not paranoia – it's reality.

And make space for your soul. A leader with no inner life will eventually run out of things to give.

As a head, you are never offstage. Pupils, staff, parents – they are reading your body language, your tone, your pace, even your shoes. You may feel this is unfair, but it's part of the deal. In a school, everyone talks about the head. Your moods, your decisions, your values, even your waistline. As a leader, you are naked. So, the question becomes: are you at peace with yourself?

Authenticity matters more than performance. Trying to imitate another head, or fit a mould, rarely works. The best leaders are those who have done the hard inner work of asking: Who am I? What do I stand for? Am I living those values, or performing them?

REFLECTIVENESS CHECKLIST

- Do I build time each day for reflection: reading, writing or stillness?
- Do I reflect regularly on how I'm using my time during a school day?

- Am I aware of my blind spots and open to discovering them?
- Do I seek honest feedback, including 360-degree reviews?
- Are my daily actions congruent with my desire to model a reflective school?
- Have I surrounded myself with colleagues who will tell me the truth?
- Am I honest about my motivations and leadership journey?
- Have I protected my personal relationships from the job?
- Do I lead with integrity, humility and curiosity?
- Am I still learning, growing and changing?

The reflective leader is not the one who has all the answers. It's the one who is willing to keep asking better questions.

And in doing so, they become not only a better leader, but a better human being.

ASIDE

WHAT MUSICAL WORK AM I?

1. I am named after the area where my composer taught – near the prestigious school that commissioned me.
2. My composer worked as Director of Music at St Paul's Girls' School for many years.
3. I feature lively dance-like movements and folk-inspired melodies, making me both educational and enjoyable to perform.
4. I belong to a tradition of English string music, similar in style to works by Vaughan Williams and Elgar, but with a distinct lightness suited for young performers.
5. I continue to be a favourite among school- and youth orchestras, reflecting my composer's lifelong passion for music education.

SAFEGUARDING

This is the only chapter in this A–Z guide where the letter choice was immediate. S is for safeguarding. To be crystal clear: if you work with children in any capacity whatsoever, your number one priority is safeguarding. No exceptions, no compromises. Not only this, but as a school leader, it is crucial that every member of staff, teaching and non-teaching, knows that this is your top priority, just as you require it to be theirs.

A recurring theme in this book is the 'flexibility' of the independent school sector and how valuable it is to consider, on a case-by-case basis, what might be best for each pupil. But none of that applies with regards to safeguarding. There is no leeway and no room for anything other than to follow – to the letter – the mandatory reporting and referral requirements pertaining to safeguarding, such as contacting the local authority designated officer (LADO) within 24 hours following an allegation against a member of staff, or the meticulous nature of your safer recruitment procedures.

Furthermore, your Single Central Register (SCR) is always accurate, complete and up-to-date.

Your Designated Safeguarding Leads (DSLs) and deputy DSLs must, therefore, not only be suitably reflective and thoughtful individuals, and undergo the appropriate training, they must also be conscientious by nature in the documenting and recording of incidents and events.

Print out a hard copy of your school's safeguarding policy. Many policies will go to 50 pages or more but, such is its importance, you should make a hard copy, and ensure you've annotated your copy with a highlighter.

As a senior leader, there should be no part of your policy that you cannot quote from.

Subscribe to an update service, so that you are fully on top of any changes or amendments to national legislation.

Lead by example. Safeguarding trumps everything. It's the mindset of every practitioner, every teacher, every member of the teaching and non-teaching staff, every senior leader.

DON'T BE ALONE

The collective knowledge and experience of independent schools is immense. You are likely to meet other DSLs on the circuit as a result of your ongoing cycle of training. But it's well worth reaching out and getting to know other DSLs in other schools and settings. In my experience, schools are generous in sharing when they have keynote speakers and on-site training. The more connected you are, the greater the chances of being invited to attend seminars and conferences.

All schools have multiple issues and concerns relating to the use of mobile phones in and out of school. National guidelines and directives are there, but it is also helpful to be able to chat with other schools about their experiences and what has, or has not, worked. Sometimes it's just so helpful to have a chat with a colleague in another setting.

PLAYGROUND SUPERVISION

Mention safeguarding and many will think of abuse or neglect and a possible child-protection issue. But the definition is far broader. For example, 'being on break duty' is a key part of safeguarding.

But because supervising pupils at break might be a regular occurrence, and because most of the time they come to no harm, there is a tendency, if left unchecked, to minimise the importance of break duty.

Being on break duty does not mean huddling together with other colleagues and drinking coffee. It is an active and serious endeavour and requires staff to be active, walking around and vigilant. It helps if senior

SAFEGUARDING

leadership are also occasionally out at breaktime, modelling the kind of attention which needs to be given.

You also want to ensure that all your staff are vigilant with regards to health and safety issues and to think of this also in terms of safeguarding. You may have workmen on your site, or you may at times notice a cable trailing, a wobbly step or a loose hinge. You want as many eyes as possible on these things.

In early years settings and in KS1, check all your doors. Time and again pupils get fingers stuck in doors, sometimes resulting in the loss of part of the finger. Hinge guards must, of course, be fitted in the appropriate classrooms. But does it happen that sometimes your youngest pupils visit other parts of the school where there are no hinge guards?

There will always be risk and one can't eliminate it completely. But you can develop a staff body which is alert to the potential for risk. Remember, safeguarding is proactive – it is everything we do to ensure that pupils aren't harmed.

KEEPING ABREAST

It's always worth reading the local newspaper. It only takes a couple of minutes to flick through it, but you'll want to be aware of everything that's happened locally to you – whether it's a cycling accident or an incident in another school. It's all part of developing a risk-aware mindset.

It's also a good idea to keep an eye on the website of the local safeguarding children's board and to read the child safeguarding reviews: lessons learned, rapid reviews and the serious case reviews as they are published.

To sum up, although your main focus is absolutely on your school, you are continually clocking the main themes and ideas in a broader base, with a view to sharpening your practice.

SUPPORT IN PLACE FOR STAFF

Always check in with staff members who are handling challenging safeguarding issues, and be prepared to provide additional support when needed. This is particularly important for form tutors, who can be deeply affected when things get heavy.

THINKING THE UNTHINKABLE

In an average week, at least four schoolchildren, some as young as ten years old, kill themselves in the UK.

Some of you reading this may have been touched by suicide. It is, of course, utterly devastating and arguably more so when it involves the death of a child. It is a real-life issue and one that a growing number of heads have faced. The toll it takes on everyone affected is incalculable.

Do not, under any circumstances, take the view that it couldn't happen in your school. If you haven't already, invest in suicide-prevention training for your staff, with the aim of developing whole-school awareness of suicide risk and mitigation – and, importantly, a common language to talk about the issue.

Papyrus Prevention of Young Suicide is the leading charity in the UK for this issue. There is an excellent free guide ('Building suicide-safer schools and colleges – a guide for teachers and staff') downloadable from their website.

Harry Biggs-Davison, a father bereaved by suicide and, also, for 26 years a headteacher in London, is today the Chair of Trustees at Papyrus. He writes:

> Although the biggest danger to children, statistically, is themselves, as suicide is their most likely cause of death, no one has told them – and their parents most probably don't know it either.

The most recent data from the Office for National Statistics (February 2025) shows that suicide rates among children were highest in households where an adult held a degree-level qualification. Conversely, households where the main adult had no formal qualifications experienced lower suicide rates.

Also of note is that boys who had SEN (special educational needs) support without a statement (such as School Action plans, Statutory

Assessment or Early Years Intervention) had the highest risk of suicide compared with those who had no recorded SEN provision.

As an educational professional, it is important that you are informed about young suicide and that you can disseminate this information throughout your school.

A NOTE ABOUT LANGUAGE

When discussing suicide, use appropriate language such as 'died by suicide' or 'took their own life.' Avoid the phrase 'committed suicide,' which comes from a time when suicide was treated as a crime — similar to how we say someone 'commits' murder. Although the law changed in the 1960s, the stigma attached to the word 'commit' is still distressing for many and makes it harder for us to talk about suicide as openly as we should. Using non-judgmental language helps reduce stigma and creates space for more open conversations about suicide.

Many young suicides are preventable. Please, let's all inform ourselves and talk about it. We can all play a role in preventing young suicide.

ASIDE
WHAT FILM AM I?

1. I am a French film released in 1970, directed by a filmmaker known for his deep interest in psychology, education and the lives of outsiders.
2. My story is based on real historical events, following the discovery of a feral child in France who had grown up in complete isolation from society.
3. Rather than being placed in a traditional school, the child is taken in by a dedicated doctor, who becomes his personal educator and guardian.
4. The boy, having lived in the wild without human contact, must be taught even the most basic elements of civilisation, such as speech, manners and emotions.
5. The educator follows the Enlightenment belief that all knowledge comes from experience and that education can shape a person's mind and soul.

TRUST

If you've ever opened a new school, then you will have had the experience of standing in front of prospective parents and pupils to talk about something that does not yet exist. The gist of your speech will be, 'Come to this school – I know you can't see it, but I'm telling you, it's going to be great and here's why …'.

Why would a parent place their child in a new school that is untested? True, they may have some faith in the credentials and experience of the founders, but it is a huge leap of faith then to commit to a new school. The same holds true if you are expanding your school upward from age 13 to GCSE, or if you are making your school co-educational, or adding a sixth form. How do you take parents with you on these journeys into the unknown?

Parents will likely not make their decision based on your welcome speech. It will come down to private conversations with you, when parents can look you in the eye, and their sixth sense decides whether or not they trust you.

Now, there are oversubscribed, famous schools where this won't be the case. The decision to send a child there has already been made. In these cases, it's more a belief that it is the right thing to do; a belief that the school will get the grades. And even if there was a change of head, it's unlikely to affect a parent's decision.

But in a small- to medium-sized school (which most independent schools are), and certainly in a new school, the decision is far more personal – it won't be a belief in your competency, but rather trust in you as a person.

Let's examine how trust functions – and how it may be fostered – across some key areas.

TRUST WITH STUDENTS

Some schools tend to be fairly relaxed places; others are run more tightly, some might say more strictly. But both can be schools with a high-trust culture, and both can be low-trust. So, what is it that determines this quality?

A recurring theme of this book is respect. Are the parents respected by the staff? Do the students respect their teachers – and do the teachers respect the students? Because if this isn't happening, you have no chance of running a school built on trust.

For students, being respected is fundamental to their wellbeing. You must create an environment where they feel secure and valued. This respect directly shapes their self-perception and emotional development – arguably for a lifetime to come. The teacher who barks, 'Get out of the way, boy!' will never understand this.

Trust develops through consistent presence, reliability and moral character. Teachers who take time to explain decisions rather than imposing them will always have their pupils onside. This is especially important with unpopular decisions. For example, I did not give permission for students who drove to school to park on school grounds. Although we had space, I took the view that we were an all-through school with little children and I was not comfortable with new drivers on the premises. I understood their frustration; they understood my reasoning.

Remarkable things happen when you prioritise building trust with your pupils. One day someone wrote, 'I hate this school' on the side of our theatre. I gathered the school, and asked that the person responsible come to see me. I was gentle and reassured them that the culprit would not be in trouble. That afternoon, a 10-year-old boy knocked on my door. In that moment, my respect for his character went up, not down. Importantly, we spoke, and I learned why he was unhappy. I didn't punish him; I didn't need to.

Of course, discipline is important and sanctions are sometimes necessary, but always in sorrow, never in anger – and always in the best interests of the student. A Spanish teacher was leading a trip to Madrid with GCSE pupils, but didn't feel comfortable taking one of the students. He sat gently with him and explained why, citing examples of behaviour that breached trust. But this was a connective conversation, not punitive – focused on growth rather than shame. The boy wasn't taken on the trip – a watershed moment for him.

A teacher might believe that a student has the cognitive ability to achieve an A*, and, if so the teacher should certainly say so. But belief is not the same as *trusting* that the student will assume the responsibility to work independently, and to follow the advice given, so belief won't necessarily translate into action. It's a useful distinction to make with students, as most of them will want to be trusted. And it's more effective than 'You are not working hard enough'!

TRUST WITH STAFF

Every head wants low staff turnover. However, authentic leadership requires genuinely wanting what's best for each member of staff – and sometimes it's the right thing for someone to move on to a new school, to a new opportunity, and we must truly be pleased for them. Fostering an atmosphere where staff tell you – in confidence – that they are tentatively exploring new roles is a two-way trust-building exercise. I never betrayed that trust, and in any case, many times the staff member stayed on.

Trust your staff to make decisions, without having to push everything further up the line. When a trivial request from a parent is met with the response 'I'll need to ask my line manager about that', it flags the low-trust environment everyone is working in. Occasionally, a less-than-ideal decision will be made, but this itself is an opportunity to reflect and learn. Such experiences should be integrated into ongoing coaching conversations, whether through structured feedback or informal discussions.

In an independent school, you really do need to trust your staff to get on with their teaching, without continually checking their work. You'll hear soon enough from the students whether they are engaged or not, and the half-term or end-of term assessment test will evidence whether they are learning anything. Heads of department will want to know what is being taught each half term, but how the teacher decides to do it should really be their business.

And every great teacher digresses from time to time, especially in response to a good question. Don't be one of those teachers that won't answer a question because it's not in the lesson plan. Over the years, we have moved ever closer to a regulated, 'professionalised' service industry, with some teachers at risk of becoming functionaries, delivering pre-scripted lessons. A far cry from the 1980s when 'Sir' would enter the class enthusing about his latest book, before pulling chalk out of his pocket and asking, 'Now, class, where were we last lesson?'.

In any case, school leaders have a responsibility to foster an interest in different approaches to teaching in varied contexts. Unleashing a diverse pool of teachers, with their eclectic mix of teaching styles and outlooks, may make life more challenging for the leadership, but from the pupils' perspective the school will seem less of a system and more a place of individuals, and thus the potential for emotional 'buy in' from pupils is greater.

So, find the right teachers who really know and love their subject and who know the exam board and what needs to be taught, then trust them to get on with it.

TRUST WITH PARENTS

Sometimes your school will make a misjudgement or get something wrong. Don't be one of those schools that 'closes ranks' or refuses to acknowledge mistakes.

The impact is profound when a school can just say, 'I'm really sorry, we got this wrong'. This shouldn't happen too often as otherwise basic competence would rightly be questioned. But building a relationship is not just about having a parents' evening. It's the ability to work through issues when things are difficult.

TRUST WITH OTHER SCHOOLS

There are obvious golden rules. Never speak badly of another school, or another head. Embrace the differences. In fact, look actively for schools that are different from yours, but which you value.

Referrals between schools must always be candid. Don't omit relevant information.

Actively build relationships with nearby schools, both state and independent. Offer an inter-school maths competition, sporting fixture or some other event to bring your schools together.

Be careful about actively 'poaching' pupils. My school was an all-through school and our pupils came to us from a variety of feeders. Traditional prep schools that go to age 13 (Year 8) now lose a good number of pupils after Year 6, and some of these preps have cut their losses and now end at Year 6. But this doesn't stop parents from sometimes asking whether their child can join your school in Year 5. It is, of course, a free market and if a parent really wants to move, and you have the space, then I suppose this can happen. But it's far better if your public line is to 'finish at your prep school before joining the senior school'.

Private, one-to-one conversations with fellow heads about the challenges and personal strains of running a school are very helpful, if only to know that you are not alone. It's important to make time professionally for those all-important lunches.

DEVELOPING A HIGH-TRUST CULTURE

Top of the agenda is developing a culture where people can speak to you candidly, and you actually know what is going on in your school. If you are head, but your leadership team never challenges you, you're likely presiding over an environment deficient in trust. Your staff may agree with their words, but they won't follow with their hearts.

When someone mentions an idea to you, do you cut them off with a 'No, that won't work'? Such responses guarantee that, eventually, innovative ideas and crucial insights will bypass you entirely.

Although you don't want to overdo it, occasionally demonstrating vulnerability by acknowledging your own mistakes and limitations to your staff can make you more human and approachable.

Once, when half-observing a lesson in reception, I absentmindedly pulled out my phone and started fiddling with it. A moment later, the teacher quietly had a word with me and asked me to put my phone away. I often referred to this incident in safeguarding briefings thereafter. I made a mistake but it certainly evidenced a high-trust culture!

ASIDE

WHO ARE WE?

1. Our story begins in the 1980s at a boarding school in England, where five students bonded over their love of music.
2. Unlike many rock bands that formed in garages, we started in a structured school environment, practising at weekends in the school's music rooms.
3. We originally named ourselves On a Friday, referencing the only day we were allowed to rehearse at school.
4. Our breakthrough came in the early 1990s with a song about teenage alienation that became an unexpected global hit.
5. We are often ranked among the most innovative and influential bands of all time, but our journey started in a prestigious independent school in Oxfordshire.

UNITY

At their best, independent schools are gloriously idiosyncratic places: a tangle of traditions, personalities, egos and enthusiasms.

As a senior leader, it's your responsibility to weave unifying strands throughout this colourful chaos. You'll be closely observed: how you interact with others, how you delight in others' interests and achievements, how you listen, as well as your openness to new ideas and others' opinions. Whether or not you can unify your school will come down to your approachability, the spring in your step, and your pride in your school and in your staff. And the twinkle in your eye.

Of course, any organisation needs some hierarchy. In certain large schools, leadership can feel like a separate class, detached from daily realities. But in small- to medium-sized schools, there's every reason to keep things relatively flat and informal. Is that headmaster plaque on your door really necessary? At heart, everyone has equal human value; you're simply playing different positions on the same team. A bit of hierarchy keeps the wheels turning, that's all.

Take a good look around at your staff, both teaching and non-teaching alike. Are you truly all in this together? Trust your gut on this one; it rarely lies. Your school will remain 'just a workplace' until everyone – from the Year 6 form tutor to the kitchen porter, the groundsman to the early years assistant– feels like a vital link in the same unbroken chain. That's when magic happens. That's when your school becomes family and when people genuinely look out for each other.

Never experienced this? Then perhaps this sounds like fluffy idealism. But if you have, you know exactly what I mean. It's when your work becomes a way of life and colleagues become your extended family. The affection you have for each other is tangible.

Unfortunately, the 'them and us' culture between staff and leadership is all too common. For example, does the common room suddenly develop an awkward silence when a member of the senior leadership team (SLT) wanders in? If so, unity is still on the to-do list.

UNITY OF PURPOSE

Why are you here? Can everyone from receptionist to football coach describe the school's purpose and its direction of travel? Those strategic goals – this year, next year, five years hence – need clear articulation. Leadership isn't just pointing the way; it's involving others, seeking their opinion, engaging their emotions.

When everyone is given a chance to grow, to take on new responsibilities, you've got something special. Because unity means getting the best from each other – unleashing talents people never knew they had. Sometimes, it's not necessary for the 'best speaker' to lead a sixth-form event; it's more important to develop all staff, helping them find their voice through assemblies and other public opportunities. The more the head can step back, and allow others to come forward, the better.

SHARED VALUES

True leadership is what happens when you're not in the room. In unified schools, teachers make decisions confidently without defaulting to 'I'll ask my line manager'. As a leader, it's for you to empower your staff to make day-to-day decisions. This becomes easier and easier when values are understood. It's a beautiful day! Why not take your class outside for a lesson? You don't need to ask permission, surely. (But maybe leave a note on the whiteboard: 'We're outside under the sycamore tree'.)

School friction typically stems from conflicting values. Consider what happens with one-to-one music lessons: students occasionally miss regular classes to attend them, which can frustrate teachers. If you're a teacher affected by these absences, try viewing them beyond just a disruptive school policy. Instead, see them as supporting an important educational goal: developing students' musical abilities. When you connect these interruptions to the school's broader aims, what feels like a personal inconvenience becomes part of a shared educational vision. This way of thinking won't solve the actual problem of students missing your class, but it helps everyone get along better by focusing on shared goals instead of conflicts.

When the staff become a family, you move from 'What's the policy?' to 'What would our values suggest?'. Your school is transformed into an entity guided by shared human principles, which become the school's values. Here, the value of properly designed school assemblies cannot be overstated. These communal gatherings create powerful moments of belonging and celebration that reinforce shared identity and purpose.

LEADERSHIP

Develop a leadership team that genuinely acts as one. Like cabinet government, debate vigorously behind closed doors, but present a unified front to your school community. And the more diverse your leadership team, the stronger it becomes. If you're an inveterate planner and controller, you need colleagues who pull you from your comfort zone – perhaps pushing a school assembly your way with no preparation time. Conversely, if you're more breezy by nature, you need team members who'll ask those uncomfortable questions about your latest brilliant idea. Your team thrives when it blends different personality types, provided you remain unified in your values – those core principles that define what matters most about your school.

A brief note about equality, diversity and inclusion (EDI): don't get completely swept away by the EDI agenda. While the sexuality, faith background or ethnicity of members of your team should never be barriers, their alignment with the school's core values remains absolutely non-negotiable.

Unity means pulling together, not having one puppet master with everyone else dangling from strings. So, mind your language: phrases like 'my staff' and 'my pupils' whisper possession when you should be proclaiming partnership. Your body language matters too: watch that you don't point at people – it's not a good look, so gesture with the open palm instead. Avoid top-down 'thou must' directives. Focus instead on influencing, nurturing and growing your team in a well-oxygenated environment that's alive with shared purpose.

Independent schools uniquely thrive on the quality of relationships rather than policies. Even as regulations multiply, this remains their distinctive edge.

Staff turnover serves as leadership's true report card; high turnover signals leadership failure. While a decent salary matters, dedicated teachers stay when they feel valued and empowered to make decisions that align with the school's moral purpose.

Is the leadership team actively mentoring colleagues, challenging them, allowing occasional failure and helping them recover? The best heads create environments where staff don't want to leave, as each day brings a sense of personal growth, and satisfies the need for acceptance and belonging.

FINAL THOUGHTS

- *Tous pour un, un pour tous.* (All for one and one for all.) Unity creates an environment where everyone strives for a shared goal. Do you feel this in your school?
- True unity requires shared values, not shared backgrounds or personalities. Cognitive diversity strengthens teams, but alignment on core values is non-negotiable.
- Leadership is what happens when you're not in the room – when staff members make confident decisions based on shared values, not fear of making mistakes.
- Unity is enacted, not imposed; it grows through relationships, trust and a shared purpose, not through policies or directives.

The head occupies a singular position – not merely at the apex, but at the very heart of school unity. They must embody the coherence they seek to create, listening widely while holding the centre firm. Every word, gesture and decision carries symbolic weight far beyond intention.

This isn't about being perfect; it's about being genuine. A leader who, with heart and soul, consistently tries to do the right thing for pupils, staff and the wider community. In the end, it's not your inspiring speeches that unify the school – it's how you live those values every single day. That's what people notice, and that's what brings a school together.

The true beneficiaries of staff unity are, of course, the pupils. Not every child grows up in a loving, stable home, but we can at least create a laughter-filled, kind, principled and consistent school environment. When staff are happy and at ease with each other, students feel it immediately – fostering a profound sense of safety, identity and confidence for everyone.

ASIDE

WHO AM I?

1. I was born in London in the late nineteenth century and attended one of England's most historic and prestigious independent schools, known for its academic excellence.
2. At this school, I was taught by one of the most famous science fiction writers of the time – someone who would later become known for stories about invisible men and time machines.
3. I wrote witty essays and humorous pieces for Punch, a satirical magazine that shaped much of British literary culture in the early twentieth century.
4. Despite my success in multiple literary genres, I am best remembered for a creation that overshadowed all my other works, something I originally wrote for my son.
5. As a lasting tribute to the school that shaped me, I bequeathed a share of my literary fortune to it, ensuring that generations of students would benefit from my success.

VOCATION

You're walking down a school corridor on a Tuesday afternoon and pass two Year 10 classrooms.

In the first, the atmosphere is calm and orderly. Students file in with quiet efficiency as the teacher, glancing between iSAMS tracking data and the whiteboard, gestures toward the day's learning objective. The lesson unfolds with practised structure: definitions, worked examples, guided practice and, finally, a short plenary quiz. The students are attentive, compliant, industrious – absorbed in the rhythm of a well-managed, professionally delivered class.

Next door the scene is different. The teacher sits informally on the edge of the desk, surrounded by unruly piles of papers. With a grin, he teases a pupil about West Ham's defeat the night before. Banter ripples through the room. Then, as if seized by sudden inspiration, the teacher leaps up, eyes gleaming, 'Can any of you imagine a world without vectors?'. In the puzzled hush that follows, he presses on, 'Imagine the pain, the confusion ...'. Grabbing a pen, he begins sketching madly across the whiteboard. This teacher has no teaching qualification, has never written a lesson plan – yet the room hums with energy. Students are laughing, questioning, thinking.

THREE KINDS OF TEACHERS

The jobber

These are the teachers whose CVs read like travel diaries. They hop from school to school with generic application letters, carelessly addressing you with the name of the previous school they applied to. They're not bad people, but they rarely move the needle. They're passing through, not putting down roots.

The professional

This group speaks fluent modern pedagogy – formative assessment, evidence-based practice, metacognition. You name it, they can talk about it. They've read Guy Claxton and John Hattie, Lucy Crehan and Pasi Sahlberg. They are dependable, diligent and career-minded, with eyes on leadership posts and alerts from the *TES* pinging on their phones. They're active on LinkedIn, union-savvy and adept at systematising practice. They shine during ISI and Ofsted inspections. You need them to run a school.

The vocational

These teachers belong. For them, teaching is not a career but a calling. You'll find them at breaktime, even when not formally on duty, playing cricket outside with the students, or kneeling beside tearful pupils searching for a missing pencil case. They're picking up litter and washing up forgotten coffee cups in the staffroom when everyone else has rushed off. They may never apply for promotion, but they hold the school's soul. They teach not just knowledge but *meaning*, and their influence is often invisible, though never inconsequential.

Most teachers embody elements of both the professional and the vocational. But at the extremes, distortions arise.

At one end is the hyper-professional: certified, data-fluent, Ofsted-praised and addicted to jargon. This is a real extract from a job application I received a few years ago:

> At the level of improving each individual learner, I have developed effective systems that use external base-line testing to set meaningful progress targets, alongside cycles of fine-grained internal, on-going assessment, moderation, data analysis, and intervention to ensure that all individuals and groups of students receive exactly the help they need as and when that need arises.

At the other extreme lies the self-proclaimed 'passionate' teacher, who declares in their application that they love their students and are adored in return. This, too, can ring hollow.

As a school leader, it's helpful to have a handle on your staff body and to understand where they are in life's journey. They could be starting out with a young family, in an unhappy marriage, managing a stressful situation with an elderly parent, or dealing with a health concern or a drink problem. What's their day like? Do they live near the school, walking or cycling in, or do they live some distance away, facing a torturous journey both ways? It's the head's job to understand a little about each staff member's story. Leadership, properly understood, begins with *attention*.

IDEALISM AND SELF-SOOTHING

We mustn't over-romanticise vocation, either. Some teachers, desperate to belong, pour themselves into school life with blinkered zeal. They work late, volunteer for every club and exhaust themselves in the quiet resentment of colleagues who don't.

Good leaders spot this pattern and guide these idealists – gently – towards sustainability, not martyrdom.

Sometimes, what we call vocation masks a deeper psychological hunger: for love, for approval, for meaning. When understood and supported, this hunger can be sublimated into extraordinary teaching. When ignored, it can curdle.

Teachers, like most people, are usually doing their best. Some are driven by ambition, some by anxiety, some by memory. Some need a secure income; others seek to change lives. A leader's task is to discern these motivations and lead accordingly.

LEADERSHIP

Leadership often begins with a longing for recognition. Few of us are so ego-less that we don't glow inside when receiving praise from colleagues, pupils or parents. But the highest form of spiritual leadership gradually becomes less about *being seen* and more about *seeing others*. It is a journey from *achievement* to *service*.

We've all encountered headteachers who speak, however unconsciously, of '*my* staff', '*my* deputy head', and so on. How different it feels when one says, '*our* deputy head', '*our* students' and '*our* community'.

The vocational leader doesn't need to trumpet personal successes – only the successes of their school community. They never speak of how brilliant or charismatic they are. They don't keep mentioning their first-class degree or other achievements. Their satisfaction comes from knowing that their day mattered; that many tiny interactions touched hearts and minds. True, their journey may have begun with seeking recognition as a fine teacher, but over time, and with growing self-awareness and wisdom, this gradually shifts toward finding joy in being part of another's journey – passing forward what their own teachers once did for them.

The values-driven head

Many heads in the independent sector are motivated by a deep sense of gratitude and duty. In some cases, they themselves were changed by a bursary or a grammar school place. They carry the torch and feel compelled to pass it on.

Some go further. It is no secret that certain heads have fallen out with their governing bodies over prioritising bursaries above new buildings. Quietly, some will go above and beyond to find funding for students in times of difficulty. Some will even call wealthy alumni and ask, 'Will you please sponsor this remarkable child?'. It's not perfect, but it speaks of real moral purpose.

Becoming a vocational leader

To those aspiring to lead, I offer this:

- **Know your people** – understand what drives them.
- **Make space for the wildcards** – the disrupters who bring edge and energy.
- **Lead with heart** – let service eclipse self.
- **Mind your language** – speak of 'our school' not 'my school'.

- **Favour substance over jargon** – champion teachers who bring their *whole* selves to their work.
- **Fight for inclusion** – be tireless in supporting bursaries and access.
- **Treasure the small moments** – that's where leadership truly happens.

In the end, vocational leadership is not about ambition or acclaim. It is about helping others flourish and finding, in their growth, the quiet satisfaction of having played your part.

ASIDE
WHAT NOVEL AM I?

1. I am a satirical novel published in 1928 by a British author known for his sharp wit and dark humour.
2. My protagonist, Paul Pennyfeather, takes a job as a schoolmaster at a shambolic, third-rate private school run by an eccentric headmaster.
3. The school is filled with grotesque and incompetent characters, from fraudulent teachers to bizarre students.
4. Through a series of misadventures, my protagonist ends up falsely imprisoned, highlighting the absurdity of fate and British society.
5. I was the debut novel of my author, who later became famous for his scathing critiques of the British upper classes.

WELLBEING

The self-confidence of any school, state or independent, emanates primarily from its belief that it is doing the right thing for its pupils.

The qualities that all great schools seek to develop are the very essence of what it means to be human: a sense of ease in oneself, an inner confidence that one's voice matters, an intellectual openness, a healthy questioning of beliefs, a capacity to love, a discovery of passions, the development of resilience and determination in the face of difficulties, a lifelong desire for continual growth and increased self-knowledge. These can't just be words – they must be at the heart of the school experience.

To this end, senior leaders must first ensure that teachers are appreciated and rewarded for how they live their lives – their own personal and interpersonal growth, and their aptitude for active listening. These are the things that need to be valued most by the leadership – much more so than the ability to deliver an outstanding lesson during an inspection, or even to secure top grades from students.

In short, it is the first responsibility of the leadership to appoint, value and retain teachers who are demonstrably self-aware and committed to further personal growth. It's nigh impossible to prioritise wellbeing within your school through various initiatives if you don't have a high proportion of reflective, emotionally healthy adults in your ecosystem.

As a school leader, particularly if you are a head, you can't fudge this. You need absolute clarity. Do you place the wellbeing of your students and your staff first – or do you prioritise results and the academic reputation of your school? And if you do place wellbeing first, are you prepared to say so publicly? Will you communicate this clearly to your school community, to prospective parents and to other schools? Will your governing body or proprietor support your commitment to what matters most?

As with all things, what matters most is congruence – not saying one thing while doing another. So, before any strategy for a whole-school wellbeing programme can be developed, it's essential to consider what you truly believe and whether this aligns with the professed vision and values of the school. Do you have the confidence to believe, by truly prioritising wellbeing throughout your school, that the results *will follow*?

STAFF FIRST

This may sound counterintuitive. After all, aren't we all there for the students? The fact is that the wellbeing of pupils and staff is deeply linked. A happy common room radiates into the classroom. Pupils intuitively sense when their teachers are tense or disconnected – and they absolutely notice how their teachers interact with each other.

You cannot meaningfully champion pupil wellbeing while quietly burning out your staff. You can't have an effective whole-school wellbeing strategy unless there is first a calm, values-driven professional environment for its adults (teaching and non-teaching staff alike).

This includes the head. Especially the head! Heads who skip holidays, reply to emails at midnight and wear their exhaustion like a badge of honour are not heroes. They are liabilities.

STUDENT WELLBEING

Take care not to see pupil wellbeing in terms of assigning mentors, putting in place counselling, safe spaces, and so on. These are important, but they are reactive. The real challenge is to design a school experience that proactively promotes wellbeing through safety and meaning.

Safety is not just freedom from bullying. It's the knowledge of knowing you are accepted as you are. It's clarity about expectations, boundaries and consequences. It's consistent and fair discipline, applied gently but firmly.

But young people also hunger for meaning. They want to know that school matters – that they matter. They want to be heard. So, ask yourself:

- Are you certain each student has a key adult they can talk to? Just assigning a tutor won't necessarily be the answer.
- Are you flexible enough, when it matters, to assign the teacher who knows the student best?
- Are your students trusted with real responsibility, or merely consulted in token gestures? If asked, where can you point to the evidence of 'pupil voice' in your school?
- Do quieter students risk slipping under the radar? Do you have a system in place to track the wellbeing of quieter students who keep their head down and stay out of trouble?
- Is your curriculum primarily a system for achieving grades? What would your students say if they were asked?

TOO MUCH ACTIVITY

We want the best for our students, but do we sometimes try just a little too hard? Ask yourself if you are over-scheduling. Sports fixtures, music ensembles, drama rehearsals, trips, clubs, lectures, debating; these all make for a rich education, but only up to a point. There is a fine line between opportunity and overload. It takes real leadership courage to say, 'Enough!'.

Your pupils don't need three cocurriculars a night. Your staff most definitely don't need another late evening. Protecting evenings, weekends, lunchtimes and holidays from institutional creep is one of the most effective wellbeing initiatives you can launch.

PARENTS

A final consideration is parental expectation. Some parents equate excellence with intensity and they clamour for more homework, more tests, more pressure.

Schools must have the courage – and the sensitivity – to educate parents. Explain the link between rest and learning, between emotional regulation and academic success. Build a shared culture where wellbeing is not a retreat from rigour but its foundation.

And when parents raise eyebrows at your decisions, hold your nerve.

CHECKLIST

- Does your school mission statement (or vision) explicitly value wellbeing above (or at least alongside) academic achievement?
- Do you demonstrate that you value staff wellbeing through your actions and decisions? Would your staff agree with your answer?
- Do you audit policies, practices and timetables through a wellbeing lens?
- Are wellbeing and emotional literacy considered as core considerations in your recruitment of new staff?
- Is wellbeing part of the DNA and culture of your school? Or is it more a collection of policies? What would your parents and students say if you asked them?

ASIDE

WHAT NOVEL AM I?

1. Published in 1972, my story follows a young man, recently returned from World War I, who takes up an unexpected career in education.
2. The protagonist, David Powlett-Jones, is a Welsh miner's son who suffers from shell shock and is advised to take a teaching post for stability.
3. Set in a traditional English public school, I explore themes of personal growth, duty and the impact of war.
4. Over time, my protagonist rises through the ranks, eventually becoming headmaster and shaping the school's future.
5. My title suggests a lifelong dedication to service, particularly in the realm of education.

XENOPHILIA

There's no 'xenophilia' in the Oxford English Dictionary, 3rd edition. But there's no reason why it shouldn't exist. If the Greek roots of the word *xenophobia* mean 'fear of/dislike of foreigners', then its opposite is *xenophilia* – 'lover of foreigners'.

And, make no mistake, independent schools are enthusiastic xenophiles. Many would have collapsed without international students, as the home market can no longer support the sector by itself. Tuition fees have tripled in the past two decades, outpacing inflation and widening the affordability gap. The middle-class family who once sent two or three children to a fee-paying school now struggles to afford to send even one.

It's no wonder, then, that schools have turned outward. The international market is booming. And British boarding schools – with their traditions, English charm and historic buildings – offer exactly the kind of prestige that many status-conscious global elites are looking for.

GLOBAL ELITES

There's nothing new in this. British schools have long educated the children of the world's royal families, diplomats and industrialists. The premise is straightforward: send your child halfway across the world to an elite school, and they'll return home with British manners, perfect English and lifelong connections.

Naturally, there's an economic benefit to the UK but arguably the real importance is the soft power it brings. Britain's soft power remains considerable throughout the world (UK ranks 2nd, behind the US and just ahead of China) – and our schools contribute significantly to this influence. One striking statistic: the UK has educated the current leaders of around one in four countries worldwide.

Meanwhile, an intense tutoring arms race has emerged as parents will do almost anything, pay almost anything, to secure their child a place at Eton or another top-flight school. As you are reading this, there are eight-year-old boys being privately tutored in Beijing and Shanghai by a small army of highly paid Oxbridge graduates, with a view to securing these boys a place further down the line. This is all about prestige – and for a wealthy international family that can afford to buy anything, their eyes are focused firmly on a handful of the most famous schools.

And for UHNW (ultra-high net worth) families, there's a perverse incentive: a scholarship is more desirable still. It's uber-wealthy one-upmanship, and money is no object. It's like a one-off piece by Balenciaga, Hermès or Cartier. Anyone can pay £60,000 a year – but to gain a scholarship is proof of excellence, prestige and good breeding. One parent asked me why a famous school cost 'only' sixty grand. 'I'd pay three times that', she said.

In this international market, the top-tier schools are now luxury brands and there's a plethora of well-connected agents and private tutors out there to help these families secure their dreams

OUR ROLE AS ADVOCATES FOR THE SECTOR

It's necessary, however, for all of us in independent education to stress – again and again – that these figures, striking as they are, are in no way representative of the independent sector as a whole, or of most families' experiences when sending their child to a prep or senior school. According to DfE figures, some 40% of all independent schools have fewer than 100 students. They don't serve the super-rich but rather focus on a local market. And yet, in the public imagination, the elite boarding school model defines the entire sector. This is a fundamental problem.

The reality is that these smaller schools don't have recruitment teams. They don't license their names abroad. They're run by local heads on modest budgets serving local families. Families who, more often than not, are making significant sacrifices to be there.

BOARDING SCHOOLS

The ISC Census 2024 shows that in that year, 26,195 international students, whose parents live overseas, were enrolled at UK independent schools. (That's up on the previous year but still down on the 29,446 pre-Covid number.) Of these, 92% attended a boarding school.

Some boarding schools now have such a high proportion of overseas pupils that they are at serious risk of losing touch with their identity. When done well, integration is, of course, enriching for everyone. But there is a tipping point. When the rugby first XV or the cricket first XI has no overseas pupils, or when Chinese students keep to themselves in separate corners of the sixth form centre, then something is lost. This is the issue that some schools are currently managing. And then the murmurs begin, 'It's not the school we signed up for'. Then, quietly, the domestic families start to leave.

This is rarely discussed openly. But when a school feels culturally unfamiliar to its host community, its roots weaken. It remains to be seen how this will play out in the years ahead.

PREPARATORY SCHOOLS

Meanwhile, in day preparatory schools, especially in London and the South East, British–Asian families now dominate – markedly so. These are not the children of global elites, but of pharmacists, doctors, accountants and small-business owners. Families who believe passionately in education as the route to success, and who are prepared to sacrifice a great deal to access it.

These are the families taking on second jobs, forgoing holidays, living in smaller homes – all to give their children a better future. For them, independent education isn't about elitism. It's about access: to better teaching, safer environments and a fair shot at a grammar school or a place at a top senior school. Their students outperform peers because they put in the hours, both in and out of school. Extra tutoring is common.

Meanwhile, the schools themselves often benefit: better results, harder-working pupils, stronger parental support. But the social fabric frays. A once-diverse community becomes oddly polarised.

A SPLINTERING SECTOR

What all of this reveals is that we can no longer speak of 'the independent sector' as a unified whole. The elite, international-facing boarding schools are playing one game. The smaller day schools in regional towns are playing quite another. Yet public policy and media coverage treat them as if they're the same.

Some schools are private businesses in all but name – catering to wealthy international families and chasing global markets. Others are struggling local schools held together by grit, charm and the goodwill of families barely clinging on.

And this matters. Because when VAT is imposed on school fees, or when political rhetoric stokes resentment toward 'private schools', it's not the big names that suffer. It's the little schools in the provinces, where VAT or a rise in fees could mean closure.

TOWARDS A THOUGHTFUL XENOPHILIA

Our overseas pupils bring much to our schools – and we should continue to welcome them. But we need, perhaps, to be a little more thoughtful. Not just about admissions, but about integration, values and long-term sustainability.

Leadership teams must ask themselves if they are always providing a rich educational experience for all their students – or simply filling beds.

This means additional investment in pastoral care and cultural onboarding. If you have international students at your school, ask yourself the following questions:

- Are your overseas students genuinely integrating into the life of your school, socially and academically, or are they forming 'parallel communities'?
- How is your school proactively celebrating and learning from cultural diversity, beyond tokenistic international days?
- Is your admissions process robust enough to assess not just academic credentials but also genuine interest in a British education, rather

than purely transactional motives (e.g. brand status, passport to university)?
- Can you discern any ethical considerations around agent use, private guardians or safeguarding?
- Do you ever turn down a student if you feel the 'fit' is not right?
- Are your overseas students at higher risk of loneliness, homesickness or mental-health issues, and how is this being monitored?
- Do your boarding-house teams and pastoral staff receive training in cross-cultural understanding, emotional literacy and the pressures these students may be under?
- Before accepting a pupil, do you *always* meet or speak with the parents (perhaps with an interpreter) or are all your interactions through an agent or through some unspecified relation?

ASIDE
WHAT FILM AM I?

1. I am a French film released in 1933, directed by an influential filmmaker known for his poetic realism and anarchic spirit.
2. My setting is a strict, repressive French boarding school where students live under harsh discipline and rigid rules.
3. The schoolmasters are authoritarian, hypocritical and sometimes grotesque, enforcing mindless obedience rather than real education.
4. I use surreal and dreamlike sequences to depict the boys' inner world, blending fantasy with reality in their acts of defiance.
5. My director, who died at age 29, drew from his own unhappy experiences at boarding school.

YESTERYEAR

When we think of the long history of the traditional English public school, particularly during its Victorian and Edwardian heyday (1837–1910), what do we think of? Well, for starters, we have bullying, fagging, flogging and cold showers. And let's not forget the emotional neglect, the stiff upper lip, spartan conditions and class snobbery. ... Yet we institutionalised and normalised this.

One shudders when one imagines how much suffering there was; how many thousands of boys had their spirits and bodies broken. And yet those that came through all this were bizarrely proud of their ability to withstand suffering, and eager to perpetuate the same. Mad dogs and Englishmen indeed.

But it can't be all bad. After all, if British education was (and is) admired the world over, there must be something about our system that is of lasting value. To this end, we preserve the house system, the importance of sports, the prefect system and the alumni network.

But perhaps there's value in looking back to the period spanning roughly 1850–1950, when these institutions were at the height of their influence, to see if there's anything else we can learn. This is not a call for uncritical nostalgia, but rather a careful examination of educational practices that might hold value for our diverse, modern educational landscape.

ORATORY, RHETORIC AND THE LOST ART OF DEBATE

While schools maintain debating clubs, few heads today would claim that teaching oratory is a central purpose of their school. Students might recognise Martin Luther King's 'I Have a Dream' speech, but rhetoric largely passes them by.

The traditional public school system once trained pupils in classical rhetorical devices, teaching them to debate logically and listen carefully. Students mastered techniques like anaphora (repeated opening phrases), chiasmus (reversed grammatical structures) and tricolon (three parallel elements); all effective tools for persuasive expression. This wasn't just an occasional lesson but a fundamental educational priority: the ability to command an audience was considered essential.

In those educational environments, oratory stood as a cornerstone rather than a peripheral activity. Students underwent rigorous training in constructing arguments, listening attentively, offering effective rebuttals and distinguishing between logical reasoning and emotional appeals.

Today's students may excel in emoji, memes and recycling opinions found online, but critical questions persist: Can they maintain well-reasoned positions when challenged? Can they engage in civil disagreement?

Could we reintroduce formal training in public speaking for all students? Few people today, outside of classically trained actors, know how to enunciate properly and use their voice. Rather than relegating debate to extracurricular activities, perhaps it deserves restoration to its rightful place in the formal curriculum. The uncomfortable truth is that most students complete university without any structured experience in speechmaking, leaving them without these crucial skills.

Perhaps formal debating, even 'declamation', and mock parliaments deserve to return – not as after-school options, but as essential training for intellectual development.

Modern speeches worth studying for their use of rhetorical devices include:

- Ronald Reagan's *Challenger* disaster TV address
- Earl Spencer's eulogy at Princess Diana's funeral
- Julia Gillard's 2012 Misogyny Speech
- Malala Yousafzai's UN Speech (2013), made on her 16th birthday.
- Oprah Winfrey's 2018 Golden Globes speech (#MeToo movement)

- Amanda Gorman's inauguration poem 'The Hill We Climb'
- Yurong Luanna Jiang's graduate address, Harvard Commencement 2025

HISTORICAL SPOTLIGHT

The Oxford Union debates of the 1930s, particularly the famous 'King and country' debate (9 February 1933) where the motion 'This House will under no circumstances fight for its King and country' passed, remind us how university debating societies directly influenced political discourse and even foreign policy perceptions.

The *Daily Express* wrote,

> There is no question but that the woozy-minded Communists, the practical jokers and the sexual indeterminates of Oxford have scored a great success in the publicity that has followed this victory. ... Even the plea of immaturity, or the irresistible passion of the undergraduate for posing, cannot excuse such a contemptible and indecent action as the passing of that resolution.

MEMORY AND RECITATION

The sad truth today is that most students, even those studying A-level English literature, will leave school without having committed any poetry to memory.

In years past, it was standard practice to learn sonnets from the canon – Shakespeare, Milton, Shelley – and passages from longer narrative poems. Today, we simply don't exercise this part of the brain as we could, or, arguably, as we should. And if students don't, or won't, engage with the classics, you can do worse than introducing them to slam-dunk poetry. Check out, for example, Joelle Taylor online.

Schools could easily revive verse-recitation competitions – again, not as a lunchtime activity or a club but as a core component of the school curriculum. Research now confirms that memorisation strengthens neural connections, enhances linguistic flexibility and nurtures the imagination.

In any event, there's a quiet dignity in knowing a sonnet by heart, or a soliloquy or two from *Hamlet*. But, like mindfulness or any other activity that one wants to introduce into a school, it does need to be modelled also by the staff. Ay, there's the rub.

SILENCE

What we sometimes forget is that the pupils of yesteryear had significantly more unstructured time to fill. There was a lot of silence – no radio, no streaming music, no headphones constantly feeding content – just silence. Time spent in chapel. Time in the library, thinking, imagining, dreaming. These empty spaces weren't seen as voids to be filled but as fertile ground for contemplation and intellectual growth.

As an educational tool, we've underestimated the value of having time and not feeling compelled to fill every moment. The modern boarding school boasts a panoply of evening events – talks, discussion groups, sports, activities; endless noise and activity. And maybe, just maybe, we've lost something along the way.

SERIOUSNESS OF TONE

In the past, education was rarely apologetic. It was serious – perhaps sometimes too serious – but never ashamed of itself. Teachers were often exacting, and often intellectually formidable. The idea that knowledge mattered – intrinsically, not instrumentally – gave the school a moral weight and purpose beyond mere utility. Somewhere along the line, there's been a shift to see knowledge necessary only so far as it's needed for an exam.

Today we make learning 'fun', but I wonder whether there's an argument to recapture the purer joy found in scholarship itself – in studying something difficult, something intricate that requires patience, stamina and seriousness of concentration. Perhaps in our rush to make education more accessible, we've sacrificed something of its essential dignity.

TIME MACHINE FUN

It's a simple matter these days to Google 'O-level maths paper 1955' and get an insight into what the past looked like. Most students today find it fascinating to see what an A-level or Scottish Higher paper from the 1930s looked like – and not least the complications that arose in maths when using pre-decimal currency. And the French and German papers expect quite an astonishing level of grammatical knowledge. Occasionally, a question might appear mildly offensive, such as this from a 1952 French paper:

> Write a conversation between an English tourist and French peasant. They discuss the peasant's work and the surrounding district.

These historical examples provide opportunities to discuss both educational standards and cultural attitudes of different eras. Students will see for themselves how knowledge expectations have shifted, sometimes becoming more specialised and sometimes more superficial.

Why not download some of these papers and take your students off-piste!

IDEAS FROM THE PAST

- **Make rhetoric central again**: build structured debate and oracy into the weekly timetable, not just as club activities.
- **Reintroduce memory work**: perhaps a poem a term, recited with flair and understanding.
- **Create space each week, especially in the prep years, for sustained reading**: designate 'deep-reading hours' with no screens, no summaries, just books.
- **Cultivate intellectual 'seriousness'**: model passion for your subject unapologetically; don't be afraid to be demanding. Reclaim the word 'scholarship'.
- **Embrace unstructured time**: allow room in the week for undirected exploration, curiosity and even boredom.

Looking to our past traditions does not mean turning back, but it may be worth glancing back, from time to time, just in case a baby went out with the bathwater.

ASIDE

WHO AM I?

1. I am a schoolteacher at an English boys' public school, where I spend nearly my entire life educating generations of students.
2. Despite my old-fashioned ways, I earn the admiration of my pupils through my warmth, humour and deep dedication to their education.
3. During wartime, I show great concern for a German teacher at the school, refusing to join in the anti-German sentiment of my colleagues and students.
4. My personal life is marked by both great love and deep sorrow, as I lose my wife, a modern and progressive woman who once inspired me to become a better teacher.
5. On my deathbed, my last words were, 'I thought I heard you saying it was a pity … pity I never had any children. But you're wrong. I have. Thousands of them … and all boys.'

ZEITGEIST

As educators, we cannot ignore the realities on the ground of the so-called 'anxious generation'. Our schools, state and independent, are by and large doing their very best to nurture young minds. Wellbeing is rightly at the top of the agenda in all schools, and yet many of our teens continue to experience unprecedented levels of psychological distress. Anxiety, depression and a generalised unease about the future have become all too common.

This book has attempted to explore some timeless educational principles, yet we must be prepared to ask whether we are just crying out in the wilderness. Can we really be sure what influences are shaping our young? The overnight success of the 2025 Netflix drama *Adolescence* speaks to our uncertainty and unease. Can we be sure that the principles discussed throughout this book remain valid in today's always-connected society, where unlimited access to both the highest achievements and darkest recesses of human depravity are just a click away? Do we really comprehend what's going on with the young today?

One thing is sure – the social frameworks we grew up with no longer suffice. It is a new world. Truth is fragile, meaning is elusive and identity is weaponised. Depressingly, we've seen this in our own education sector. The school labels 'private' and 'state' threaten to polarise and spark further infighting at precisely the moment when we should unite around our common purpose: doing our absolute best for young people in an unstable world.

While I have no fixed political affiliation, having voted for all the major parties in my time, we cannot ignore the current government's hostility toward the independent sector. Education Secretary Bridget Phillipson

MP, who should represent the educational interests of *all* children, made her position unmistakably clear just months into her tenure:

> @bphillipsonMP
>
> Our state schools need teachers more than private schools need embossed stationery.
>
> Our children need mental health support more than private schools need new pools.
>
> Our students need careers advice more than private schools need AstroTurf pitches.

The condescending reference to embossed stationery undermines the dedicated work of thousands of teachers, classroom assistants and support staff throughout the independent sector. It particularly overlooks specialised SEND provision that has transformed the lives of students whose needs were often inadequately addressed within the state system.

The independent sector remains eager for partnerships, with extensive expertise and global connections that could benefit all if co-operation were prioritised over ideology.

Yet the government has refused engagement while actively working to diminish the sector's influence – precisely when collaboration is most needed. The suspension of Eton College's partnership with Star Academies exemplifies how ideology has overridden potential student benefits, depriving young people of life-changing educational pathways through a world-class sixth-form programme that would have positively impacted the wider community.

IMMEDIATE CHALLENGES

1. **Political and financial pressures – a Darwinian landscape**: The imposition of VAT on school fees, and loss of business rate relief, represents a real threat to many schools. But the persistent 93%/7% rhetoric means that most voters remain unconcerned with the struggles of independent schools. Surviving this storm will require many schools to urgently re-examine their business models – perhaps reducing provision or implementing hybrid-learning

systems. For many, the imperative is clear: innovate and adapt, or perish.

2. **Affordability**: The days when the local doctor or solicitor automatically sent their children to an independent school are over. The numbers just don't add up anymore. For years, fees have risen faster than incomes, and the pool of families who can afford independent education is shrinking before our eyes.

   Right now, we're seeing leaner competitors breaking onto the scene, providing a streamlined educational experience with reduced extracurricular offerings. These schools are leveraging the advantages of blended-learning models and flipped classroom approaches to control costs. This pragmatic adaptation, borne of economic reality, may turn out in time to revolutionise the way children learn, especially since adaptive AI technology is just getting started. One certainty remains – parents still want independent education for their children, but many are baulking at the premium prices being charged.

3. **Demographics and shifting markets**: Declining birth rates across many regions aren't doing independent schools any favours. Schools face tougher competition for a shrinking pool of fee-paying families, especially if they're outside Surrey or the major cities. To stay ahead, schools really need to get strategic and embrace data-driven approaches to make the most of their domestic markets. Overseas students are quite literally a lifeline – for both day schools and boarding schools.

4. **Why independent education?**: Parents are asking themselves whether independent education is, in fact, worth it. Top-performing (albeit selective) state schools often outperform independents, so results alone are not a good enough reason. For those parents seeking traditional school experiences for their children, the likely deciding factors will be demonstrable added value and superior pastoral care. Schools need to work much harder to showcase what truly makes them special. Those governing bodies which just coast along or adopt a 'wait-and-see' approach will see their days numbered.

5. **Widening access and social responsibility**: The provision of means-tested bursaries and genuine community outreach are an essential part of the independent sector's legitimacy. Parents want their schools to be socially responsible and a preparation for 'the real world'.

6. **Staff recruitment**: Attracting and retaining great teachers is tougher than ever, particularly in maths, physics and languages. First-class, British-style international schools are increasingly attracting talented teachers in search of adventure (and thus away from the UK local market). Staff are more vocal about wanting good working conditions. The days of expecting staff to simply 'make do' are over.

7. **AI and the future**: There is a growing realisation that the tsunami of AI has not yet hit. But already, it is evident that current practices will be uprooted by the new technology that many practitioners are only just beginning to get to grips with. There's widespread dissatisfaction with traditional assessment models and curriculum approaches. Everyone seems agreed that change is needed but that is likely to take time. In the meantime, there's an opportunity for schools to exercise their independence to take market share through innovation and effective communication of their ethos and values.

THE EDUCATIONAL ZEITGEIST

While undeniably a period of upheaval, this moment also offers conditions for reinvention. The best schools (including some of the smaller ones) – nimble, self-aware and mission-driven – are seizing the moment not merely to survive but to lead: by contributing to policy debates, pioneering new models of learning and redefining what excellence in education might look like for the twenty-first century.

The *Zeitgeist* is one of anxious transition – but it is not without hope, especially given the presence of so many inspirational, thoughtful and entrepreneurial leaders throughout the sector. Those schools that can reconcile tradition with transformation may well emerge not diminished, but renewed.

> ## ASIDE
> ### WHAT NOVEL AM I?
> 1. My story follows three boys – Ralph, Jack and Peterkin – who are stranded on a deserted island.
> 2. My characters build shelter, find food and create a kind of utopian existence in the wilderness.
> 3. I am often seen as a prototype for later survival and adventure novels, including *Lord of the Flies*.
> 4. My author was known for writing books aimed at young readers, often emphasising moral values.
> 5. My title refers to the idyllic, tropical setting where my young heroes must learn to survive.

SECTION TWO

POLITICS AND INDEPENDENT EDUCATION

None of us would deny that our democracy is richer and stronger for having political parties that represent different strands of conservatism, liberalism and socialism. But no book about independent school leadership can sidestep the issue that the UK Labour Party has a long history of opposition to independent education. This is from the 1983 general election manifesto:

> Private schools are a major obstacle to a free and fair education system, able to serve the needs of the whole community. We will abolish the Assisted Places Scheme and local authority place buying; and we will phase out, as quickly as possible, boarding allowances paid to government personnel for their children to attend private schools, whilst ensuring secure accommodation for children needing residential education.
>
> We shall also withdraw charitable status from private schools and all their other public subsidies and tax privileges. We will also charge VAT on the fees paid to such schools; phase out fee charging; and integrate private schools within the local authority sector where necessary. Special schools for handicapped pupils will retain all current support and tax advantages.

It could be argued that the independent sector has had 40 years' notice of Labour's intention to add VAT to tuition fees. And while a few familiar faces, eloquent advocates for independent education, pop up occasionally on television and in the media, the inescapable reality is that the sector *as a whole* has failed to make a strong enough representation with the general public. This despite the exceptional partnership work of many individual schools. Somehow the message just isn't getting out. This is something for us all to ponder.

How extraordinarily powerful it would be if only we could harness the nation's collective education expertise and experience, bringing together schools of different kinds from both state and independent sectors for the good of society and the benefit of all children.

HISTORICAL PERSPECTIVE

State education received unprecedented investment and underwent significant reform and modernisation during the Blair years (1997–2007). While the Assisted Places Scheme was discontinued, the Blair government invested substantially in state–independent sector partnership projects. This period of partnership may have created a false sense of security within the independent sector that ultimately delayed necessary adaptation to changing social attitudes. The independent sector was experiencing growth, boosted by a buoyant economy, and there was perhaps a misplaced assumption that cross-party support would continue indefinitely.

It's as if the independent sector was thinking, 'We are at the centre of everything, and even the Labour Party is supporting us!'.

The educational landscape evolved gradually but doggedly over subsequent years, through the coalition government and into Conservative administrations. Social priorities shifted, with equality, diversity and inclusion becoming central concerns, alongside questions about access to Oxbridge and broader discussions about educational privilege. These conversations emerged from across the political spectrum, not exclusively from the left.

The independent sector had opportunities to demonstrate leadership in key educational areas, but arguably failed to contribute meaningfully to national conversations about SEND, oracy, curriculum development and provision for looked-after children – with boarding-school provision quite possibly an underexplored area – potentially fertile ground for leadership within the sector.

At present, the sector is barely present in national conversations about the future of education in this country. A collaborative approach – strengthening ties with local state schools, learning from successful partnership models like the School Partnerships Alliance and participating more actively in national educational dialogue – is the way forward.

Meanwhile, the prestigious schools with substantial resources will undoubtedly continue pioneering innovative private–public partnerships to support disadvantaged teenagers. We need advocates across the country speaking about their commitment to unity and serving all children. And those serving the public good need to be cheered on.

THE VAT ISSUE IN 2025

On 1 January 2025, all independent-school fees in the UK became subject to VAT at the standard rate of 20%. This was a key pledge in the Labour Party's 2024 General Election manifesto. The stated aim was to fund the recruitment of 6500 new teachers in the state sector. The party's position was that 'asking the public to subsidise a tax break for private schools is inexcusable'.

This characterisation appeared consistently in ministerial communications and treasury press releases, where the term 'tax break' was frequently used to describe the previous VAT exemption.

In late December 2024, HM Treasury posted the following on X (formerly Twitter):

> @hmtreasury
>
> On 1 January, the 20% VAT break for private school fees will come to an end, enabling better investment in state education and helping recruit 6,500 new teachers.

Numerous commentators from within and beyond the education sector questioned the framing of the VAT exemption as a 'tax break'. Timothy Straker KC, Joint Head of Chambers at 4–5 Gray's Inn Square, in a letter to *The Times* (3 January 2025), offered this analysis:

> VAT replaced purchase tax on 1 April 1973. That tax had itemised goods or services subject to it; education was never taxed. VAT was formulated differently and imposed on goods and services at large. Consequently, it was necessary to schedule goods and services to be exempt. Education was, like medicine, one such service. That exemption has now been varied so that school fees

(but not, for example, university fees) are subject to VAT. I have not heard it suggested that those paying university fees are ... enjoying a tax break.

The ISC and others argued that this change, particularly in how it was communicated, mischaracterised how VAT functions. VAT is a consumption tax paid by the consumer – in this case, parents – not by the schools themselves. Yet the media narrative was that schools were enjoying a 'tax break'.

LEGAL CHALLENGE

In April 2025, three linked judicial review claims reached the High Court, challenging the government's policy decision to add 20% VAT to school fees. The claimants – a group that included pupils, their parents, and four schools – argued that the move was incompatible with the European Convention on Human Rights (ECHR).

These families, supported by the Independent Schools Council (ISC), had chosen independent schools for specific, personal reasons: children with special educational needs (but without formal EHCPs), pupils requiring faith-based education, or girls needing single-sex schooling for safeguarding reasons – including those who had previously experienced sexual harassment. Their legal team pointed to Article 2 of the First Protocol, which guarantees the right to education, and Article 14, which prohibits discrimination in the enjoyment of that right.

At the heart of the argument was this: the new VAT policy wouldn't affect all families equally. It would hit some particularly hard – especially those already on the margins. For children with additional needs, for whom mainstream provision simply wasn't working, or for parents whose religious or safety concerns shaped their educational choices, the financial barrier could be life-changing.

But in June 2025, the High Court disagreed. In *ALR and others v Chancellor of the Exchequer*, the judges dismissed all three claims. While they accepted that the VAT policy would make private education unaffordable for some families, and that it might disproportionately affect particular groups, they concluded that the resulting discrimination was legally justified. Governments, the judges said, enjoy broad discretion in matters of taxation and social policy – particularly when acting on a manifesto commitment.

An appeal is still a possibility but the bar is high. The court's ruling underlined just how reluctant judges are to interfere with fiscal policy unless the legal case is overwhelmingly strong. And as things stand, it's clear that threshold hasn't been met.

WIDER CONTEXT

The removal of VAT exemption for independent schools has not been introduced in isolation. In parallel, the government also withdrew business rates relief from charitable independent schools in England. This move followed similar decisions in Scotland (2022) and proposals in Wales.

Charitable schools do not operate for the benefit of shareholders, and any surplus is ploughed back into the school – which needs to evidence its charitable purpose, not least through the provision of bursaries to children who would otherwise be unable to attend. Nonetheless, all independent schools, regardless of whether they are charitable or for-profit entities, are now subject to VAT on fees.

This has created a notable inconsistency in the application of VAT to education: while private pre-school education, private tutoring and university fees remain VAT-exempt, primary and secondary independent education do not. We now have a two-tier approach to VAT in education based on pupil age rather than provider type:

- Private nursery education: VAT is not applied to fees.
- Private primary education: VAT is applied to fees.
- Private secondary education: VAT is applied to fees.
- Tertiary education: VAT is not applied to fees.

The loose and misleading use of language has irked the independent sector. The debate around the loaded phrase 'tax break' highlights how language can shape public understanding of government policy.

As this policy becomes established, its consequences will become clearer. Some schools, especially smaller or lower-cost providers, are facing insurmountable challenges, with closures being announced on a weekly basis: 18 independent schools announced closure plans in the first three months of 2025. This trajectory is likely to continue as more middle-income families find themselves unable to access a sector they previously could afford.

Beyond the immediate financial impact, this legislation raises fundamental questions about educational choice, access and the relationship between state and independent sectors, as well as the reputation of the UK globally as a beacon of educational excellence.

Right now, the sector needs leadership, not a 'wait-and-see attitude'. We need the kind of leadership that captures airwaves, that can weave a story and engage constructively with all parties of whatever political persuasion. It's time to demonstrate that the sector's contribution to British education strengthens rather than divides our educational landscape.

SLEEP – THE CASE FOR LATER SCHOOL STARTS

Remember your teenage years? That strange ability to stay wide awake into the small hours while struggling to form coherent sentences before 9am.

During adolescence, something fascinating happens to the human body clock. Teenagers experience what scientists call a 'circadian shift' – their biological rhythms move later, causing them to feel sleepy and wake up about three hours later than children or adults. As Professor Russell Foster, a leading research scientist at Oxford University, puts it: 'Teenagers are essentially living in another time zone. Having teenagers get up for school at 7am is like asking adults to wake at 4am.'

Despite what some old-school teachers might think, this isn't about laziness or poor habits – it's biology. The teenage brain experiences a delayed release of melatonin (the sleep hormone) from the pineal gland. This natural neurodevelopmental process clashes dramatically with the typical early school-start times.

Given the compelling scientific findings, the question for all school leaders is to consider whether there is a case for allowing older teenagers, say sixth-formers, to start school an hour or two later in the day. Anecdotal evidence suggests that starting later has a profound effect on sleep, mood and concentration.

THE TEENAGE CIRCADIAN SHIFT

- Adolescents lose an average of 2.7 hours of sleep on school days due to this biological clock mismatch.

- By Thursday or Friday, many teenagers are under-slept by a staggering 12–14 hours.
- This chronic sleep deprivation affects learning, emotional regulation, decision-making and overall health.

We all know what sleep deprivation does to us as adults – now imagine functioning that way as your default state while also navigating the challenging waters of modern adolescence.

THE REAL IMPACT

Sleep isn't just about feeling rested. It's the greatest cognitive enhancer we have – the fuel that makes our brains efficient. When teenagers operate on insufficient sleep, the consequences ripple through every aspect of their lives:

- **Cognitive function**: reduced concentration, memory and learning capacity
- **Emotional wellbeing**: increased irritability, stress and vulnerability to depression
- **Physical health**: suppressed immunity and stronger correlation with obesity
- **Decision-making**: poorer choices regarding alcohol, driving and other risky behaviours
- **Relationships**: strained interactions with peers, teachers and family.

While it's true that late-night screen time exacerbates sleep problems, it's important to note that this is an aggravating factor, not the root cause of the circadian shift itself.

THE CASE FOR LATER STARTS

The educational research community is virtually unanimous: later school starts for adolescents would positively impact learning, health and safety. The question is whether such a change can be implemented in the context of your school.

Some years ago, Oxford University's Teensleep Project tried to recruit state schools into a research programme but none would bite. In the independent sector, a number of schools have successfully implemented later starts. Among the benefits are:

- improved student wellbeing and concentration
- better retention of existing students transitioning to sixth form
- increased attraction of students from other schools.

Interestingly, these schools have discovered an unexpected marketing advantage – the later start becomes a distinctive and attractive feature of their sixth-form offering.

Context is essential, and what works brilliantly in one school might not translate to another. This isn't about imposing a one-size-fits-all solution, but rather inviting school leaders to examine the evidence and consider their unique circumstances.

Could a later start time – even by just one hour – make a difference to your older students? The accumulated research suggests it's a question worth exploring.

FINANCIAL COMPETENCY FOR INDEPENDENT SCHOOL LEADERS

In today's climate, a head must be both financially astute and entrepreneurially agile.

Most heads and senior leaders come from academic or pastoral routes and haven't had formal training in finance, yet are expected to oversee multi-million-pound operations with financial and strategic responsibility. Thankfully, it's never been easier for a determined head to develop their financial literacy.

The *Financial Times Guide to Finance for Non-Financial Managers* by Jo Haigh (2011) is one of many excellent introductions. Alternatively, all the basics, such as the balance sheet, the income statement and the cash-flow statement, can be learned through some excellent videos readily found on YouTube (though best to stick to explanations relevant to the UK).

Today's most successful heads combine educational vision with financial know-how; they are always keeping an eye on costs, and always seeking to improve their financial understanding. Heads must have a clear vision of what they seek to achieve, but light-touch adjustments might need to be made along the way to keep the right balance between vision and viability, between being mission-driven and financially-responsible.

Effective conversations with your bursar depend on speaking their language. You don't need to become a financial expert, but you must know enough to ask insightful questions and evaluate the answers.

Career opportunities increase when you demonstrate both educational *and financial* expertise. This combination will set you apart from many other candidates during interviews.

COMPANIES HOUSE AND THE CHARITY COMMISSION

Understanding where and how your school reports its finances provides valuable insights. Practise interpreting financial statements by researching nearby schools and downloading their accounts from Companies House (if they're limited companies) or from the Charity Commission website (if they're registered charities).

A school's public name may differ from its legally registered name, so check both when researching.

Charity Commission reports are typically more detailed and informative. They contain a trustees' annual report, including total fee income, other income and staff costs, as well as information on public benefit activities, such as bursaries and outreach.

Companies House filings are generally shorter, but nevertheless you'll see the total fee income, staff costs and profitability, including shareholders' dividends. You will see significant differences in, for example, the ratio between fee income and staff costs in different schools. All interesting information!

If your school is part of a private-equity- or venture-capital-backed group, examining the holding company's accounts is essential to gain a true picture of the school's financial security. A school that appears healthy locally may be vulnerable if the group is over-leveraged or facing cashflow pressures.

ABOUT DEPOSITS

Know your total deposit liability. In a school of 300 pupils, each having paid a £1000 deposit, you're holding £300,000 that *belongs to parents*. Assuming pupil numbers remain stable, this gives you a healthy operational float – but those funds must be properly recorded as a liability on the balance sheet, not quietly absorbed into general cashflow.

Review your terms and conditions regarding deposits. This is perhaps cheeky, but some schools specify that deposits are repayable when a pupil leaves the school 'upon request' and even 'returned two months after leaving' which can help manage cashflow during the summer. Some parents will, in fact, forget to request the return of the deposit. Occasionally, a parent will want to donate it to the bursary fund.

Be transparent about unclaimed deposits. Consider making it clear in your terms and conditions that unclaimed deposits will be donated to your bursary fund. If so, ensure these funds are properly allocated.

MARKET AWARENESS OF SCHOOL FEES

Monitor competitor fee levels once they're publicly announced (but never discuss planned increases with other schools – this violates competition law).

Understand what you're comparing. Check whether published fees include lunches, activities or other extras. It can be a fiddly process to gather all the information, but having a clear sense of what your competition is doing is key to positioning your school effectively.

EBITDA

Teach yourself to calculate EBITDA (Earnings Before Interest, Taxes, Depreciation and Amortisation). While this isn't the final word in running your school accounts, tracking your operational efficiency and profitability over time will provide valuable insight into whether your school business is improving year on year. If your school operates as a limited company and you're (discreetly) considering mergers or acquisitions, EBITDA will be a key figure in your valuation discussions.

Financial literacy combined with an entrepreneurial mindset will redefine your leadership and help secure your school's future.

- **Deepen your conversations with your governing body or proprietor.** Watch their confidence grow as you demonstrate command of both educational strategy and the financial roadmap to achieve it.
- **Move from reactive to proactive leadership.** Instead of responding to financial constraints, anticipate challenges and create new opportunities.
- **Build a culture of financial awareness.** As your self-assurance develops, you'll naturally cultivate financial responsibility throughout your leadership team. Get used to negotiating prices – for everything.

- **Prepare for the unexpected**. What happens if you start the new school year with ten fewer families? What is your break-even number? If necessary, what action can you reasonably take to reduce costs if you have a sudden fall in pupils?

To sum up, the broad mechanics of running your independent school are relatively straightforward. First, you sit on deposits which, in principle, provide a valuable buffer and float for day-to-day operations. Second, unlike many businesses, parents pay up front, with three clear cash-injection periods each year. You have many fixed costs (staff salaries, pensions, etc.) and your enrolment should be relatively stable – with the important term's notice clause providing some budgeting stability.

Against all this, your high fixed costs mean that even losing a small number of students can push your school into the red. Keeping an overall eye on your fee-income-to-staff-costs ratio will help you weather storms; the downside is that parents may well notice if you have one teaching assistant too few in your lower years. You will have to weigh up greater financial stability (i.e. a greater buffer) versus possible reputational damage.

CODA

Governing bodies and proprietors don't always recognise that effective school leadership directly contributes to staff stability. Since recruiting new staff is both expensive and time-consuming, prioritising staff retention represents one of a head's key financial imperatives.

In short, leading your independent school is an infinitely complex kaleidoscope of activity, where each moving part can impact both your reputation and cashflow significantly.

This is the heart of independent school leadership. Financial vigilance isn't just about protecting your bottom line; it's about creating the stability that allows your educational vision to flourish. The schools that master this delicate balance don't just survive – they adapt and thrive, whatever the challenges; they define excellence for generations to come.

ANSWERS TO ASIDES

WHO AM I? WHAT AM I?

A: Miss Grayling in the *Malory Towers* series (1946–51) by Enid Blyton

B: Jonty Driver (1939–2023), Master of Wellington College (1989–2000)

C: Anna Freud (1895–1982), a key figure in psychoanalytic child psychology

D: Wackford Squeers, owner and headmaster of Dotheboys Hall, in *Nicholas Nickleby* (1839) by Charles Dickens

E: 'Galloping Foxley' in *Someone Like You* (1953) by Roald Dahl

F: W. Somerset Maugham (1874–1965), novelist, playwright and short-story writer

G: Geoffrey Fisher, Headmaster of Repton School (1914–32) and Archbishop of Canterbury (1945–61)

H: A.S. Neill (1883–1973), founder of Summerhill School

I: *Forty Years On* (1968) by Alan Bennett (b. 1934)

J: John Keating (played by Robin Williams) in *Dead Poets Society* (1989)

K: Maria Montessori (1870–1952), Italian educator

L: *The Browning Version* (1948), by Terence Rattigan (1911–77)

M: John Locke (1632–1704), philosopher

N: Leo Tolstoy (1828–1910), novelist and educator

O: Kurt Hahn (1886–1974), German educator

P: Lev Vygotsky (1896–1934), Russian psychologist

Q: *The Prime of Miss Jean Brodie* (1961), by Muriel Spark

R: *Brook Green Suite* (1933), by Gustav Holst

S: *L'Enfant Sauvage* (The Wild Child, 1970) dir. François Truffaut

T: Radiohead

U: A.A. Milne (1882–1956), who left one-quarter share of the copyright of his Winnie-the-Pooh books to Westminster School. This request remains the largest legacy to the school to this day and has funded numerous scholarships and bursaries.

V: *Decline and Fall* (1928) by Evelyn Waugh

W: *To Serve Them All My Days* (1972) by R.F. Delderfield

X: *Zéro de Conduite* (Zero for Conduct, 1933), dir. Jean Vigo

Y: Mr Chips in *Goodbye, Mr Chips* (1934) by James Hilton

Z: *The Coral Island* (1857) by R.M. Ballantyne

REFERENCES

Albery, N. (ed.) (1994). *Poem for the Day: One*. London: Chatto & Windus.

Allen, D. (2015). *Getting Things Done: The art of stress-free productivity*. London: Piatkus.

Aurelius, M. (2006). *Meditations*. Translated by M. Hammond. London: Penguin Classics.

Birbalsingh, K. (2025). 'The questions Bridget Phillipson must answer about Labour's Schools Bill'. *The Spectator*. Available at: www.spectator.co.uk/article/the-questions-bridget-phillipson-must-answer-about-labours-schools-bill/

Covey, S.R. (1989). *The 7 Habits of Highly Effective People: 30th anniversary edition*. London: Simon & Schuster UK Ltd.

Department for Education (2014). 'Early years foundation stage (EYFS) statutory framework'. Available at: www.gov.uk/government/publications/early-years-foundation-stage-framework–2

Department for Education (2024). 'Behaviour in Schools: Advice for headteachers and school staff'. Available at: assets.publishing.service.gov.uk/media/65ce3721e1bdec001a3221fe/Behaviour_in_schools_-_advice_for_headteachers_and_school_staff_Feb_2024.pdf

Drucker, P.F. (1966). *The Effective Executive*. New York: Harper & Row Publishers.

Gov.uk (2003). 'Every child matters'. Available at: www.gov.uk/government/publications/every-child-matters

Haigh, J. (2011). *The Financial Times Guide to Finance for Non-Financial Managers*. Harlow: Pearson Education Limited.

Independent Schools Council (2024). 'ISC census and annual report'. Available at: www.isc.co.uk/media/uukn4r3i/isc_census_2024_15may24.pdf

Kennedy, B.H. (1962). *Shorter Latin Primer*. Essex: Longman.

Labour Party Manifesto (1983): Available at: www.labour-party.org.uk/manifestos/1983/1983-labour-manifesto.shtml

Lazear, J. (1992). *Meditations for Men Who Do Too Much*. A Fireside/Parkside Meditation Book. New York: Fireside.

Office for National Statistics (2025). 'Risk factors for suicide in children and young people in England'. Available at: www.ons.gov.uk/peoplepopulationandcommunity/healthandsocialcare/mentalhealth/articles/riskfactorsforsuicideinchildrenandyoungpeopleinengland/2025-02-27

Paterson, J. and Macnaughton, E. (1938). *The Approach to Latin: First part*. Edinburgh: Oliver and Boyd.

R (ALR and others) v Chancellor of the Exchequer (2025). 'Press Summary: For release at 10am, 13 June 2025'. Available at: www.judiciary.uk/wp-content/uploads/2025/06/ALR-and-others-v-Chancellor-of-the-Exchequer-private-schools-VAT-judgment-PRESS-SUMMARY.pdf

Rawls, J. (1971). *A Theory of Justice*. Cambridge, MA: Belknap Press.

Sayers, D.L. (1947). 'The lost tools of learning'. A paper read at a vacation course in education, Oxford 1947, 11.

Tidy, H. and Irving-Walton, J. (2024). '#LTHEchat 282: Quirky Teaching in Higher Education'. #LTHEchat. Available at: https://lthechat.com/2024/01/12/lthechat-282-quirky-teaching-in-higher-education/

Wilson Schaef, A. (2004). *Meditations for Women Who Do Too Much*. Revised edn. New York: HarperOne.

FURTHER READING

Allen, D. and Lamont E. (2024). *Team: getting things done with others.* London: Piatkus.

Allen, D., Williams, M. and Wallace, M. (2018). *Getting Things Done for Teens: Take control of your life in a distracting world.* London: Piatkus.

Benson, A.C. (1908). *The Schoolmaster: A commentary upon the aims and methods of an assistant-master in a public school.* London: John Murray.

Berry, J. (2016). *Making the Leap: Moving from deputy to head.* Carmarthen: Crown House Publishing.

Blatchford, R. (2014). *The Restless School.* Woodbridge: John Catt Educational Ltd.

Claxton, G. (2008). *What's the Point of School?: Rediscovering the heart of education.* Oxford: Oneworld Publications.

Coates, M. (2023). *The Relentless Pursuit of Peace: A roadmap to mental health.* London: The School of Educational Leadership.

Collen, I. (2020). *Language Trends 2020.* British Council. Available at: www.britishcouncil.org/sites/default/files/language_trends_2020_0.pdf

Crehan, L. (2016). *Cleverlands: The secrets behind the success of the world's education superpowers.* London: Unbound.

Davies, J. and Stephen, M. (2021). *An Overseas Parent's Guide to UK Education.* St Albans: RSL Educational Ltd.

Dix, P. (2017). *When the Adults Change, Everything Changes: Seismic shifts in school behaviour.* Carmarthen: Independent Thinking Press.

Elliot Major, L. and Briant, E. (2023). *Equity in Education: Levelling the playing field of learning – a practical guide for teachers.* Woodbridge: John Catt Educational Ltd.

Eyre, D. (2016). *High Performance Learning: How to become a world class school.* Abingdon: Routledge.

Gosling, M. (2025). *Teenagers: The Evidence Base*. London: Swift Press

Haidt, J. (2024). *The Anxious Generation*. London: Penguin.

Hammond, A. (2015). *Teaching for Motivation*. Woodbridge: John Catt Educational Ltd.

Handy, C. and Aitken, R. (1990). *Understanding Schools as Organizations*. London: Penguin Business.

Handy, C. (1999). *Understanding Organizations*. 4th edn. London: Penguin Books.

Hawkes, N. (2013). *From My Heart: Transforming lives through values*. Carmarthen: Independent Thinking Press.

House of Commons Library, 4 October 2024. 'Independent schools: taxation and charitable status'. Available at: https://researchbriefings.files.parliament.uk/documents/SN05222/SN05222.pdf

James, D. and Lunnon, J. (2024). *Schools of Thought*. London: Bloomsbury.

James, R. (2022). *Chess for Schools: From simple strategy games to clubs and competitions*. Carmarthen: Crown House Publishing.

Jamison, K.R. (2011). *Night Falls Fast: Understanding suicide*. London: Picador.

Kelley, P. and Griffiths, S. (2018). *Body Clocks: The biology of time for sleep, education and work*. Woodbridge: John Catt Educational Ltd.

Kelley, P. and Lee, C. (n.d.). 'Later education start times in adolescence: Time for change'. Education Commission of the States. Available at: www.ecs.org/clearinghouse/01/12/19/11219.pdf

Labour's fiscal plan (n.d.). Available at: https://labour.org.uk/change/labours-fiscal-plan/

Lewis, R.D. (2018). *When Cultures Collide: Leading across cultures*. 4th edn. London: Nicholas Brealey International.

Lockley, S.W. and Foster, R.G. (2012). *Sleep: A very short introduction*. Oxford: Oxford University Press.

O'Connor, R. (2018). *When it is Darkest: Why people die by suicide and what we can do to prevent it*. London: Vermilion.

Rae, J. (1993). *Delusions of Grandeur: A Headmaster's Life*, 1966-86. London: HarperCollins.

Rhodes, J. (2015). *Instrumental: A Memoir of Madness*, Medication and Music. Edinburgh: Canongate.

RSAcademics (2023). *The New Art of Headship.* Available at: www.rsacademics.com/the-new-art-of-headship-report/

Seldon, A. (2009). *Trust: How we lost it and how to get it back*. London: Biteback Publishing.

Tate, N. (2023). *What is Education for?: The views of the great thinkers and their relevance today*. London: Bloomsbury Academic.

Thomas, G. (2021). *Education: A very short introduction*. 2nd edn. Oxford: Oxford University Press.

The A–Z series focuses on the 'fun and fundamentals' of what's happening in primary, special and secondary schools today. Each title is written by a leading practitioner, adopting a series approach of reflection, advice and provocation.

As a group of authors with a strong belief in the power of education to shape and change young people's lives, we hope teachers and leaders in the UK and internationally enjoy what we have to say.

Roy Blatchford, series editor

The A–Z of Great Classrooms (2023)

The A–Z of Secondary Leadership (2023)

The A–Z of Primary Maths (2024)

The A–Z of School Improvement (2024)

The A–Z of Diversity and Inclusion (2024)

The A–Z of Trust Leadership (2024)

The A–Z of International School Leadership (2024)

The A–Z of Special Educational Needs (2024)

The A–Z of Early Career Teaching (2024)

The A–Z of Student Wellbeing (2025)

The A–Z of Addressing Disadvantage (2025)

The A–Z of Independent School Leadership (2025)

The A–Z of Primary English (2025)

The A–Z of Good Governance (forthcoming)

The A–Z of Primary Leadership (forthcoming)

Personalised professional development from Hachette Learning Academy

A simple way to boost career progression, staff motivation and educational excellence.

Our online courses are:

 Aligned with **teaching competency frameworks**

 Written by experts in education, including Hachette Learning authors (formerly John Catt)

 Created to enable educators to **develop competencies** linked to their professional development aspirations

 Powered by adaptive learning, to accommodate a diverse range of skills, knowledge and understanding

 Designed to support **effective learning and high-impact teaching**

www.hachettelearning.com/academy